THE KETO COOKBOOK

Innovative Delicious Meals for Staying on the Ketogenic Diet

Dawn Marie Martenz

Laura Cramp, RD, LD, CNSC

demosHEALTH

New York

Visit our website at www.demoshealth.com

ISBN: 978-1-936303036
E-book ISBN: 9781617050930

Acquisitions Editor: Noreen Henson
Compositor: diacriTech
Printer: Bang Printing

Medical information provided by Demos Health, in the absence of a visit with a healthcare professional, must be considered as an educational service only. This book is not designed to replace a physician's independent judgment about the appropriateness or risks of a procedure of therapy for a given patient. Our purpose is to provide you with information that will help you make your own healthcare decisions.

The information and opinions provided here are believed to be accurate and sound, based on the best judgment available to the authors, editors, and publisher, but readers who fail to consult appropriate health authorities assume the risk of injuries. The publisher is not responsible for errors or omissions. The editors and publisher welcome any reader to report to the publisher any discrepancies or inaccuracies noticed.

CIP data is available from the Library of Congress

Special discounts on bulk quantities of Demos Medical Publishing books are available to corporations, professional associations, pharmaceutical companies, health care organizations, and other qualifying groups. For details, please contact:

Special Sales Department
Demos Medical Publishing
11 West 42nd Street, 15th Floor
New York, NY 10036
Phone: 800-532-8663 or 212-683-0072
Fax: 212-941-7842
E-mail: specialsales@demosmedpub.com

Made in the United States of America

13 14 / 5 4

Contents

Foreword

The ketogenic diet has a storied history. While its introduction in modern neurology for use in the treatment of epilepsy is typically attributed to Dr. Samuel Livingston in Baltimore, even Dr. Livingston describes a reference to fasting to cure seizures from the Bible in his book published in 1963, *Living with Epileptic Seizures.*

Dr. Livingston's successor as the Physician-in-Charge of The Johns Hopkins Hospital Epilepsy Clinic was Dr. John M. Freeman. Dr. Freeman essentially resurrected the diet as a standard treatment for at least medically intractable epilepsy during the second half of his career when he redirected his attention from aspects of birth defects and ethics to a concentration in pediatric epilepsy. His book *The Ketogenic Diet*, written with his Hopkins colleagues Eileen "Patty" Vining, M.D., and the late (and beloved) Diana Pillas, served as an important guide for parents of children with epilepsy. Dr. Freeman trained many leading child neurologists including Eric Kossoff, M.D., who has continued clinical studies of the ketogenic diet and widened its use, including extension to the idiopathic epilepsies, for example, absence epilepsy, and variations on the diet, specifically the "modified Atkins" diet.

The mechanism of the diet's effects remains elusive, although neuroscientists have been actively researching this question. The diet has been determined to be a targeted therapy for certain disorders, specifically glucose transporter deficiency (where the diet provides an alternative to glucose as fuel for the brain), and pyruvate dehydrogenase complex deficiency (where the diet provides for an alternative pathway for the mitochondria to produce energy). Yet metabolic disorders in general represent a minefield where the ketogenic diet can inadvertently worsen an underlying metabolic defect and convert a patient from relative stability to rapid deterioration. Hence, the diet is not a "natural alternative" for epilepsy and is at least as complicated as taking a drug in terms of the ramifications that can ensue for the body's metabolism.

The diet can be unpleasant and unappetizing and this has been a longstanding concern among physicians and parents. But, at long last, one patient's extremely talented mother brought her love and caring into play, making the ketogenic diet attractive and even delicious. It has been my privilege to work with Mrs. Dawn Martenz and her outstanding family in the epilepsy genetics program at Children's National Medical Center. We decided at a particular point of frustration during her child's

v

treatment that a trial of the diet, although not necessarily considered typical for a child with her daughter Charlotte's diagnosis, Dravet syndrome, would be worth the effort. None of us predicted that the outcome would be a series of recipes and culinary creations that could indeed be considered so appealing, if not delectable, as to warrant this unique cookbook. Together with our outstanding ketogenic team, including Drs. Tammy Tsuchida, Tesfaye Zelleke, and Amy Kao, Mrs. Martenz teamed up with Laura Cramp, R.D., a dietitian who, as in other centers, evolves as the key ingredient of the ketogenic diet clinic. Together they produced this outstanding cookbook that will be among the greatest assets of any family facing the dilemma of using dietary therapy to treat their child's epilepsy. My hat is off to these authors, and those families, for the fantastic efforts – and results – that come with this work.

Phillip L. Pearl, MD
Chief, Division of Child Neurology
Children's National Medical Center
Professor of Pediatrics, Neurology, and Music
The George Washington University of Medicine
     and Columbian College of Arts and Sciences
Washington, DC

Appropriate Adminstration and Potiential Complications of the Ketogenic Diet

Amy Kao, MD

The ketogenic diet may have less obvious side effects than medications, but it has its own set of possible problems and should be treated just like an anti-seizure medication. The family and patient should talk with their neurologist about whether the ketogenic diet might be a good treatment option. Then, the neurologist should refer the patient to a specialized team involving a dietitian and another neurologist who have expertise and experience in managing patients on the ketogenic diet. This team should review the ketogenic diet in detail with the family, confirm that the patient is a good candidate for the diet, prepare the family for initiation, supervise the start of the diet, and communicate with and see the family frequently throughout the time the ketogenic diet is being used, just as when a medication is prescribed.

There are some problems that can occur, especially during the start of the ketogenic diet. Because of these possible problems, patients are admitted to the hospital for initiation of the ketogenic diet, so that monitoring for symptoms and frequent blood work can be done.

HYPOGLYCEMIA (LOW BLOOD SUGAR)

In general, blood sugars are relatively low on the ketogenic diet, but if caloric needs are not calculated properly, they can get dangerously low and cause symptoms such as sleepiness, vomiting, nervousness, trembling, and sweatiness. In such cases, a certain amount of sugar given in the form of apple juice or unflavored Pedialyte®, or even intravenous fluids (without sugar), might be necessary.

EXCESSIVE ACIDOSIS (THE BLOOD IS TOO ACIDIC)

Again, in general, the acidity of the blood is relatively high while on the ketogenic diet due to the acidity of ketones. However, if it is too acidic, there may be symptoms such as panting, irritability, increased heart rate, facial flushing, unusual fatigue, and vomiting. A certain amount of juice or unflavored Pedialyte® or intravenous fluids might be needed. If the level stays low, additional bicarbonate might be prescribed as a daily medication to balance out the acidity. This is a common complication when starting the ketogenic diet, but usually resolves after a short period of time if the patient remains well hydrated.

DEHYDRATION

Thirst can decrease and urination can increase while on the ketogenic diet, leading to a risk of dehydration. If there are signs of dehydration, blood sugar, ketone levels, and acidity need to be checked and additional fluids given. Dehydration can also cause or worsen constipation.

ENCEPHALOPATHY

If excessive fatigue or decreased responsiveness occurs, or the patient just is not acting like him- or herself, low blood sugar, excessive acidosis, or dehydration could be the cause. The ketogenic diet can cause an increase in some antiseizure medication levels, such as phenobarbital, which could also cause sleepiness. In addition, the ketogenic diet could worsen an undiagnosed underlying metabolic disorder, thereby leading to a change in behavior.

After hospital initiation of the ketogenic diet, parents and patients are asked to check blood sugars and blood or urine ketones periodically at home. In addition, they meet with the dietitian and neurologist frequently for outpatient visits to monitor for problems that can happen while on the ketogenic diet long term.

CONSTIPATION

This is not an unexpected side effect from such a high-fat, low-fiber, and relatively low-fluid diet, but can be an uncomfortable problem for some patients. It can be managed by increasing fluids and certain foods like avocado or low glycemic vegetables, as well as by providing daily stool softening medications. If constipation is not managed well, it can lead to decreased appetite, which in turn can cause poor growth and low blood sugars.

GROWTH ISSUES

The restrictiveness of the ketogenic diet necessitates consultation with a registered dietitian to help determine nutritional needs. These needs will change over time and frequent visits to the dietitian and ketogenic diet team are required to ensure appropriate growth. Weight and height are measured at every visit, and caloric intake is calculated, with the goal of maintaining adequate growth but not excessive weight gain or loss. The dietitian also considers several other factors, such as ketone levels, seizure control, level of hunger, and activity level when making changes in the ratio of the diet, the amount of protein, or the number of calories.

HYPERLIPIDEMIA (ELEVATED CHOLESTEROL)

Several blood tests are also checked at every visit to look for side effects that do not show obvious signs or symptoms. Cholesterol and triglycerides are often mildly elevated and, if levels are of concern, can be addressed by increasing polyunsaturated fats, adding fish oils, or decreasing the ratio of the diet. Patients who have a family history of hyperlipidemia occurring at a young age are at higher risk for this issue.

NUTRITIONAL DEFICIENCIES

The ketogenic diet is, in general, relatively low in certain vitamins and minerals. Prepared products or formulas such as Ketocal®, however, include a multivitamin supplement. A sugar-free multivitamin and a calcium supplement with vitamin D is recommended for all patients on the ketogenic diet who do not use large amounts of these prepared products. Levels of specific vitamins, minerals, and other compounds are routinely checked, including calcium, magnesium, phosphorus, vitamin A, vitamin D, vitamin E, zinc, selenium, and carnitine. Deficiencies in these may contribute to problems such as decreased bone density/osteoporosis and cardiomyopathy (abnormality of the heart muscle). We also check fatty acid lipid panels, which include omega-3 and omega-6 levels. Supplements or dietary changes may be needed if certain levels are abnormal.

KIDNEY STONES

Patients who have a family history of kidney stones, or are on certain medications such as topiramate or zonisamide, are especially at risk for kidney stones. Avoiding dehydration or excessive acidosis while on the ketogenic diet minimizes this risk.

In general, most patients who are on the ketogenic diet do well without complications or may experience side effects that are tolerable or manageable. Just as with antiseizure medications, patients are seen frequently and laboratory tests are performed routinely in order to ensure that the benefits outweigh the side effects.

Acknowledgments

Although this book only has two authors, there are dozens of people who have contributed to it whom we would like to thank. First, we thank the many parents and children on the ketogenic diet at Children's National Medical Center. You inspire us to work hard every day to provide this diet and to continually improve *how* we provide it. By sharing your experiences, ideas, and recipes, you have benefited the entire neurology community. We would also like to thank Beth Zupec-Kania, R.D., for allowing us to use her KetoCalculator program to create these recipes and for educating and promoting the ketogenic diet to hundreds of dietitians and families.

We would also like to thank the following people:

Tammy Tsuchida, MD, PhD, ketogenic diet neurologist at Children's National Medical Center. We gratefully acknowledge Dr. Tsuchida's review of this manuscript and for her tireless contributions to our ketogenic diet program and the care of our patients. She has spent countless hours caring for the patients and supporting just about everything we have wanted to do to change and improve our program. She is greatly missed as the ketogenic diet neurologist and her contributions to the program will continue to benefit every child that begins the diet at CNMC.

Amy Kao, MD, and Tesfaye Zelleke, MD, ketogenic diet neurologists at Children's National Medical Center. They are both immensely supportive of and dedicated to the ketogenic diet program and bettering the lives of our patients.

Philip Pearl, MD, Division Chief of Child Neurology at Children's National Medical Center who has specifically cared for and improved Charlotte's life through better seizure control.

OVERVIEW

How to Use This Book

This book is unlike any other cookbook. The ketogenic diet is a medical diet and can be harmful to your health if it is not followed correctly. A neurologist and a dietitian are necessary ingredients in each one of these recipes; without them, you cannot safely and successfully follow the ketogenic diet.

You can use most recipes you find in a cookbook just as they are described, using the ingredients listed in the amounts indicated. For the recipes in *this* book, however, you must consult a dietitian and neurologist to guide you in how to adjust these recipes to fit your needs. Each child has different calorie and fat needs to promote appropriate growth and to control seizures. You will notice that each recipe has blank spaces next to the gram amounts for each ingredient. Use these spaces to enter your specific gram amounts as prescribed by your dietitian.

Every meal recipe you will find in this book is about 400 calories and contains at least 8 grams of protein, with one exception: The Yogurt Parfait recipe contains only 2.9 grams of protein. Every snack and dessert is approximately 150 calories, but varies in the amount of protein it contains. Also, every recipe is a 4:1 ratio (4 grams of fat for every 1 gram of protein and carbohydrate combined). We chose these numbers because, when combined into three meals and two snacks, they create a meal plan that is common among school-age children on the ketogenic diet. This calorie level does not meet the needs of every child on the ketogenic diet, but with the help of your dietitian, you will be able to adjust the proportions without much difficulty to fit your own dietary needs.

You will also notice that each of the recipes contains a carbohydrate amount (rounded to the nearest 0.1 gram). Although this information is not necessary for the ketogenic diet, it can be helpful in the Modified Atkins Diet. These recipes can be used to supplement the Modified Atkins Diet, but as with the ketogenic diet, you must work with a dietitian to ensure that your child's diet is nutritionally adequate and sustainable.

Another benefit to these recipes is that each one of them is gluten-free. The specific brands have been checked for potential gluten-containing ingredients, but please keep in mind that ingredients may change over time. Please check the label of the specific foods you are using if you want to maintain a gluten-free diet.

MEAL PREPARATION TECHNIQUES

A common concern among caregivers is how they are going to cook a separate keto meal along with a family meal when time is already tight. Planning ahead is the best way to incorporate the same ingredients into both the family meal and the keto meal. However, this may not always be possible on a regular basis. It can be helpful to have a supply of pre-made meals and ingredients frozen and clearly labeled for future use. A few preparation methods will help streamline the process of cooking multiple batches at once.

Cooking with the Same Protein as the Family Meal

Ketogenic meals can be quickly prepared alongside a typical dinner preparation. Not only does incorporating the same protein into the keto meal help the child feel included, it also reduces time and waste in the kitchen. Cook the main protein for your family dinner without any added seasonings or sauces. Remove the needed keto portion, then continue to cook the family meal, seasoning as desired.

Before leaving the hospital, make sure you have recipes that include the same types of protein that your family is used to eating. If keto meal plans call for 85% ground beef, and your family is used to 90% lean beef or diced sirloin, ask to change the recipes right away.

Assembly Line Method

This is the technique you would use to create multiple batches of a meal that includes ingredients that *cannot* be blended together, such as the Bake and Freeze Pizza. You can easily create and then bake multiple pizzas at one time. Simply line the ingredients up on the counter top and prepare one meal from start to finish, using the same mixing bowls and utensils, then repeat.

When a recipe calls for an ingredient such as beaten egg whites, it is helpful to make a large batch of egg whites and then prepare several of the meals that call for that ingredient. When melted butter or coconut oil is called for, you can melt a large amount and weigh each portion using a medicine syringe, add it to the recipe, and move on to the next ingredient.

All-in-One Batch Method

This method can only be used when all of the ingredients are *completely* blended together, such as the Chocolate Popsicles, Waffles and Brazil Nut Cookies. In this method, you would multiply each ingredient weight by the number of servings that you plan on making. Next, weigh all of the ingredients and mix together very well, making certain that all the ingredients are evenly distributed. Lastly, figure out the total weight of each serving. For example, the recipe for Chocolate Popsicles for six servings would look like this:

50 g avocado	$50 \text{ g} \times 6 = 300 \text{ g}$
6 g bakers chocolate, unsweetened	$6 \text{ g} \times 6 = 36 \text{ g}$
4 g coconut oil	$4 \text{ g} \times 6 = 24 \text{ g}$
3.5 g truvia™	$3.5 \text{ g} \times 6 = 21 \text{ g}$

The total weight of the recipe is found by adding the weight of each ingredient together; in this case:

$$300 \text{ g} + 36 \text{ g} + 24 \text{ g} + 21 \text{ g} = 381 \text{ g total weight}$$

Next, divide the total weight by the number of servings and you have found the weight for *each* serving:

$$381 \text{ g} \div 6 = 63.5 \text{ g for each serving}$$

To double check that your math is correct, the weight for each serving should equal the total number of grams (all ingredients added together) for the original recipe:

$$50 \text{ g} + 6 \text{ g} + 4 \text{ g} + 3.5 \text{ g} = 63.5 \text{ g}$$

Weigh each portion in the container in which it will be stored and cook or freeze accordingly.

SYMBOLS

Most of the recipes contain symbols that describe certain features of that recipe. Use these as a guide for choosing meals and snacks that meet your child's needs.

Symbols Chart

Symbols	Name	Meaning
	Grab and Go	Travels well
	Complete Bite	Every bite has the same diet ratio; good for picky eaters or "grazers"
	Selenium	Recipe contains at least 30 mcg selenium
	Quick	Recipe can be made in less than 15 minutes
	Smooth Consistency	Soft/smooth consistency, good for infants or oral aversions
	Vegetarian	No meat or fish, may contain dairy and/ or egg
	Fiber	Recipe contains at least 5 grams of fiber
	Finger Food	No utensils needed
	Freeze	Freezes well

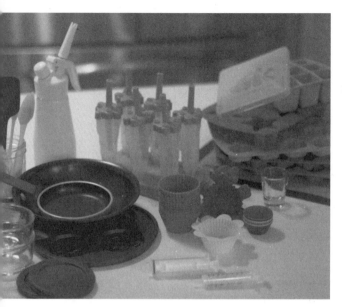 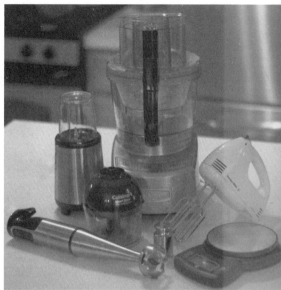

EQUIPMENT AND UTENSILS

You will notice that specific types of kitchen items are used on a regular basis in this book. Preparing ketogenic meals requires accuracy, smaller-scaled utensils and cookware, and non-stick surfaces such as silicone muffin liners, parchment paper, and non-stick frying pans. This helps to ensure that all of the ingredients go from scale to cookware to serving plate without losing portions of the weighed ingredients, which would alter the ratio of the diet.

The goal while preparing keto foods is to have as few utensil exchanges as possible between the food preparation and the actual serving of the food. Minimizing the contact of food on mixing bowls, plates, and utensils helps ensure that all of the weighed ingredients are eaten in the proper ratio. One to two grams of fat can quickly be lost if a frying pan is not scraped out *very* well after cooking.

Following is a discussion of essential keto supplies and a few non-essential items that help make the diet more fun and kid friendly.

Digital Gram Scale

This is only required item to buy *before* starting the diet. You will want to be sure you understand how to use your specific scale before leaving the hospital. We recommend that all families have at least two scales because digital scales can be fragile and can break easily! They are often hard to find in retail stores and most often are purchased on-line. Find out if the keto center that you will be using provides a scale. If they do not, The Charlie Foundation sells a 1,000-g capacity scale that is recommended for use on the ketogenic diet. Having a large capacity scale such as this allows ample room to weigh ingredients *and* a vessel to hold them in. For example, a 2-cup glass measuring cup weighs nearly 621 grams! If you have purchased a 200-g scale because it was less expensive, you will have a difficult time weighing food in this container. A less expensive, lower capacity scale can be purchased as a back-up scale, but a high capacity scale is very helpful for everyday food preparation.

Practice good habits when using the scale. It is important to use a calibration weight on a weekly basis. This will alert you if the scale has become uncalibrated because of moving it around or possibly because of low battery life. Also, most scales come with protective covers that should be used whenever the scale is not in use. This hard, plastic cover will protect the scale's sensors from damage. It's very easy to permanently damage the sensors — just pressing too hard on the scale or weighing something too heavy will cause damage. Again, always replace the cover when the scale is not in use. It is often helpful to reserve a small area on the kitchen counter for the scale and as the keto food prep area. This eliminates the need to move the scale around and therefore lessens the chance of damaging or dropping the scale. Lastly, always have a supply of batteries for your scale, even if you are in the habit of using the AC adapter; you will be inconvenienced should the power go out.

Keep the receipt and the box that the scale was packaged in when purchased. Many scales have an extended warranty and you will need the receipt for any warranty repairs. Familiarize yourself with the manual and proper operating and handling methods. Make it very clear to children in the household that it is not a toy and should only be used by an adult. Also, the scale is best protected in its original packaging for traveling and family trips.

Without your scale, *you cannot prepare ketogenic food properly or safely for your child.* Your scale is the most important tool in your kitchen for administering the diet and should be handled correctly at all times.

Small Silicone Spatulas

These are used for scraping the sides of bowls and plates to ensure getting every drop of fat. The silicone flexes easily and does not melt, making it ideal for frying or sautéing. Progressive International sells a set of 6-inch silicone spatulas for about $6.00. These are a great size for kids; they can easily fit in small mouths to help get every last gram of food in.

Silicone Muffin Liners/Baking Mats

Many meals and snacks are cooked in muffin liners because there is no chance of losing fat during the cooking process. These are washable and re-usable, and can be baked, microwaved, and frozen. Wilton Industries sells many different varieties of these, some of which are pictured in this book, which will help make meals more appealing to kids.

Silicone baking mats are flat sheets of silicone designed to cover a metal baking sheet. These are ideal for baking or freezing items that you would like to be bite size, such as the Jell-O® Puffs or the No-Bake Chocolate Snack Bars.

Electric Hand Mixer

Small, inexpensive hand mixers with removable beaters make quick work of beating egg whites, emulsifying fats, or whipping the heavy cream. They are very inexpensive and can often be found in grocery stores.

Immersion Blender/Blender

This will help blend or puree small amounts of food. Some families also use Magic Bullet™ blenders because they use small cups to both blend the food and use as a serving cup, so little food is lost during the blending process.

iSi® Easy Whip

This is a tool that is used in professional kitchens to make whipped cream instantly. If you find that your child likes whipped cream and you whip cream often, this tool is worth the investment. You can now find models designed for home use in kitchen supply stores. To use, fill the canister with heavy cream and screw the lid on tightly. The canister must be charged with a nitrogen cartridge. Next, squeeze the handle and dispense perfectly whipped cream. This cream is light and fluffy, making the volume appear much greater than cream whipped with an electric mixer. You can dispense just a few grams at a time right into a serving bowl. The canister can be stored in the refrigerator until all of the cream is used.

Food Processor

A full-size food processor will work great for making nut butters, grinding nuts, or pureeing large batches of food; however, a mini food processor may be even more useful. The mini versions are just about the perfect size for keto meal batches; they are less expensive and they have fewer parts to clean. A mini food processor will work just as well as a larger model; just be sure you do not overheat the motor!

Silicone Candy Molds

Silicone candy molds can be used for many purposes: to freeze pre-weighed coconut oil or butter, bake cookies, make freezer bars, or even to freeze pre-cooked or pre-measured ingredients for meals. Because they are extremely flexible, you can completely remove all of the contents while they are frozen solid. For baking purposes, fat will not be absorbed into the silicone, making them ideal for baking cookies or making coconut oil/butter candies.

They also come in many different shapes and sizes, making it easy to provide your child with holiday themed or seasonal shaped cookies and snacks. You can find many varieties of the molds in craft stores in the baking departments.

1-Ounce Glass Measuring Cups/10-ml Syringes

A 1-ounce glass measuring cup is very handy for weighing or serving oil. It is small enough to accommodate the needed oil, but not so big that you are left with a large area from which to scrape the fat. It is re-usable, dishwasher safe, and economical — about $1.00 each in large chain stores.

Another way to measure and serve fat is 10-ml or sometimes even 20-ml syringes. This eliminates the need to drink oil from a cup or to scrape a bowl clean. Some kids actually respond quite well to taking the oil in a similar fashion to taking medicine. If this works for your child, it will help make the meals overall less greasy and oily. These have the advantage of also traveling well; some syringes come with a small cap to prevent leakage, which is ideal for packing a lunch bag or for eating meals outside of the home.

For families preferring a disposable container to store fat or small meals, 1-ounce condiment cups also work well. These can be purchased in bulk at membership clubs such as Costco or Sam's Club. The lids and cups are often sold separately.

Non-Stick Frying Pan

A small non-stick frying pan dedicated to keto meal preparation is essential. A heavy pan will help ensure that the food does not burn or stick. Remember, if any portion of the meal has burned or becomes stuck to the pan during the cooking process, the meal cannot be served because you have *lost* weighed portions of the ingredients and have changed the overall ratio of the meal.

Depending upon your child's calorie level, a small 6-inch pan may be best suited for meal preparation. This ensures that there is not too much surface area of the pan in relation to the amount of food being cooked, lessening the potential of losing or burning ingredients.

A separate pan for keto meals allows the keto meal to be cooked alongside the family meal, minimizing the chance of non-keto–friendly ingredients, such as sauces and flavorings, coming into contact with the keto meal.

SPECIFIC FOODS

Heavy Whipping Cream

The recipes in this book use 40% heavy whipping cream. There are several types of heavy whipping cream available in most grocery stores and knowing the difference is important. The percentage refers to the amount of milk fat in the cream. If you can only find 36% heavy whipping cream, let your dietitian know so he/she can modify the recipes to include your specific cream. Please use the chart below to help differentiate between creams.

Cream Chart

	40% Cream	36% Cream
Serving size	15 ml	15 ml
Calories	60	50
Grams of fat	6	5

Butter

You will also notice that the recipes contain European butter. This butter is slightly different than regular American butter in that European butter contains up to 84% butterfat (regular butter contains up to 80% butterfat). It can be found in most grocery stores. Regular butter can also be used, but you will need a few more grams, so remember to recalculate accordingly.

Ghee (Clarified Butter)

Ghee is a butter that has been pre-heated to remove any moisture and milk proteins from the butter. This results in butter that is 100% butterfat, making it equivalent to oil. All butters made from cow's milk, especially ghee, are very high in cholesterol.

Oils

All oils are equal in their content of fat (100% fat), but each has different nutritional properties. Vegetable oils do not contain cholesterol, but do contain varying amounts of saturated fats.

Coconut oil and palm kernel oil have some of the highest amounts of saturated fat. Walnut oil, flaxseed oil, soybean oil, and safflower oil all have high amounts of polyunsaturated fat, which can lower cholesterol levels.

There is one type of oil, medium chain triglyceride (MCT) oil, which is directly absorbed into the blood and does not require digestion. Because of this, it increases the body's level of ketosis and can help make the diet more effective. It can also result in stomach cramping and diarrhea, so it should be consumed in small amounts and increased slowly as tolerated. With the help of your dietitian, you can decide if MCT oil should be included in your child's diet and how much should be added at a time.

Oil sprays can be helpful when a recipe calls for something to be cooked prior to measuring. A light spray of oil in a pan can be used to cook meat, sauté vegetables, or even scramble an egg.

Remember, not all oils can be used for frying. The best options for frying are soybean oil, canola oil, and corn oil. Unrefined walnut oil, coconut oil, and flaxseed oil should not be used for frying due to their relatively low smoke points. In general, unrefined oils are not safe for cooking and the refined versions should be used whenever there is heat involved.

Mayonnaise

Recently, many brands have started producing healthy alternatives to mayonnaise. These products usually reduce the overall fat content and may result in larger amounts of mayonnaise needed in the recipe. In this book, we opted to use regular mayonnaise to reduce the amount needed to meet the diet ratio and to preserve the overall palatability of the meal.

Nuts

All nuts can be ground in a food processor to create "butter" or "flour." If you use these ingredients often, it may be helpful to grind them in large batches and store in an air-tight container, away from sunlight. All nuts should be fairly shelf stable, but will last longer if kept in the refrigerator or out of sunlight. You can also find commercial nut butters and nut flours in most grocery stores, but remember to always check for added ingredients. Brazil nuts are highest in selenium; almonds are high in protein, but not as high as peanuts. Macadamia nuts and pecans are highest in fat, and cashews are the highest in carbohydrates.

Sweeteners

Many artificial and natural sweeteners are labeled as calorie free. Generally, when a sweetener is in a powder form, there is a small amount of carbohydrate that is not accounted for on the label. The liquid forms of these sweeteners may be a better option to reduce the amount of uncalculated carbohydrate consumed. Truvia™ is used in many of the recipes in this book, but you will notice that it is calculated into the recipe to account for the small amount of carbohydrate it contains. Any calorie-free sweetener can be used in place of Truvia™, just be sure to adjust the calculations.

Some families have noticed that certain artificial sweeteners can be a trigger for seizures or behavioral changes. Keep this in mind when starting the diet or if you are not able to achieve optimal seizure control. Sweeteners should be used sparingly; your child will gradually adjust to accepting the natural sweetness in foods after not eating large amounts of sugar for a time. Try to use as little added sweetener as possible.

Spices and Flavorings

Pure extracts are considered a "free food" on the ketogenic diet. Also, flavorings such as those from Bickford Flavors are also a free food because they do not contribute to the nutritional content of the meals. This does not mean that you can use as much of them as you want whenever you want. Limit the use of flavors, including sweeteners, to 15 drops per day. Some people can tolerate higher amounts, but for the uncontrolled child, it is best to minimize the use of these products. If more than a pinch of any seasoning is desired, it must be calculated into the meal plan.

Spices such as cinnamon, oregano, salt, and pepper are also "free foods." These can be helpful in adding flavor to meals, making them more palatable. Try to limit these to a "pinch" per meal.

Protein

Almost all of the recipes call for pre-cooked meats, poultry, and fish. This is designed make meal preparation faster and easier. Batches of meats and poultry can be sautéed using spray oil or baked on a silicone baking sheet and then placed in freezer bags and frozen until just before use. Chop the meat into bite size pieces before freezing so that you can easily remove a small amount for each meal.

We have also used minimal amounts of processed meats such as bacon, hot dogs, and deli meats. This is to reduce the amount of fillers, preservatives, and nitrates. Some families have found that these too can be triggers for seizures or behavioral changes.

Whipping

When a recipe calls for whipped cream or whipped egg whites, always whip first and then measure. If the egg or cream is measured before whipping, some of the quantity will be lost on the mixer.

Whole Foods

It is always best to choose *whole* foods when preparing keto meals. Foods such as chips, chicken patties, hot dogs, French fries, and other processed foods are generally seen as high in fat, but are not keto-friendly due to the fillers and *types* of fat they contain. Choosing fresh or frozen fruit and vegetables and whole meats, poultry, and fish will allow you to use more of these ingredients and may help decrease the amount of "bad" fats in your diet, such as trans fat. Also, similar to the processed meats and artificial sweeteners discussed earlier, some families have found that processed foods can be a trigger for seizures or behavioral changes and should be avoided early in the ketogenic diet process.

Beverages

The ketogenic diet does not contain very much liquid, so most people on the diet need to drink extra fluid to meet their hydration needs. This is especially important to help avoid kidney stones. Water is always the best option for hydration, but if your child does not like plain water there are other options for meeting fluid needs. You can usually buy seltzer water or soda already flavored from most grocery stores. Be sure to check the label to make sure it is calorie and carbohydrate free and does not contain a sweetener to which your child is sensitive. You can also purchase them without flavoring and use extracts and artificial sweeteners to flavor at home. Brew your own herbal, caffeine-free tea at home and serve either hot or cold. If your child prefers sweet tea, you can use an artificial sweetener to sweeten. You can also add water to the cream or almond/coconut milk that is already calculated into your recipes. If a recipe calls for 20 grams of cream, add water or soda water to it to create "milk" or "cream soda."

Charlotte's Story

A MOTHER'S PERSPECTIVE

Charlotte was born on May 12, 2005, a healthy full-term infant. The day after her four-month vaccinations, she woke up from her morning nap and her right arm was jerking. I knew instantly that she was having a seizure. I called 9-1-1 and we were taken to our local emergency department in Nashua, New Hampshire. That first seizure lasted 45 minutes until it was stopped with medication in the emergency department. We were sent home only a few hours later with the understanding that it was a febrile seizure. Three months to the day later, it happened again. We called 9-1-1 and went to the emergency department once again, but this time, as there was no fever and it was her second seizure, we were transferred to Boston Children's Hospital. We stayed there for three days while the doctors ran every test they could think of. At seven months old, Charlotte endured two spinal taps, an MRI with sedation an EEG and EKG, a heart ultrasound and kidney ultrasound, and a 24-hour urine catheter. All tests were negative. We were sent home with Diastat® and training about how to stop her seizures ourselves. Charlotte was also started on phenobarbital. Over the next five months she had three more seizures. A few weeks after her first birthday, we found out that we were expecting our second child. Charlotte continued to have seizures every few months—they had turned into full tonic-clonic seizures—and we had started seeing a pediatric neurologist. It was everyone's opinion that we were dealing with normal childhood epilepsy, but at about 18 months old, I noticed that Charlotte would look up toward the sky as if she was watching an airplane. During that summer, we had started her on Trileptal® and her seizures become much worse. She began seizing several times a week and was turning blue with each seizure. My mother and mother-in-law both had to perform rescue breathing during a seizure for her while babysitting. We all became very scared to be alone with her. On one panicked phone call to her neurologist, I asked if her seizures were some kind of terrible childhood syndrome, not just idiopathic epilepsy. They assured me that she was fine, and it would be very rare for her to have a genetic seizure disorder. As it turned out, her eye deviations toward the sky were the onset of her myoclonic seizures. My instinct told me that this was not just "run of the mill" epilepsy.

About six weeks before I was due to have our second baby, we saw a new pediatric neurologist at Dartmouth Hitchcock Medical Center in New Hampshire. He agreed to genetic testing.

15

On February 11, 2007, our son JT was born. We were home with him for just 24 hours, when we had to go back to the NICU because of jaundice. While we were there, he started vomiting and the doctor took an x-ray and found that his intestines were distended from a possible bowel obstruction, and they thought it was possible it could rupture. We were immediately put on a transfer back to Dartmouth Hitchcock for emergency surgery. When JT and I arrived at 4 a.m., the surgeon decided that they had time to do a few tests before proceeding with an operation. While I sat and waited for biopsies and x-rays, I made a panicked phone call to Charlotte's neurologist's office in the same hospital. I had myself convinced that JT was going to have the same problems as Charlotte even though his symptoms were not at all similar. I also knew that the genetic test results for Charlotte should have been back by then and I was determined to get the same screenings for JT, fearing the worst. Later, Charlotte's neurologist came to the NICU and I asked him immediately if he had the results. Our search for the cause of all the seizures had come to an end; she had Dravet's syndrome.

This was the lowest of all our lows, and Charlotte's neurologist clearly did not want to give me this terrible diagnosis during all of the instability with JT. He told me not to worry and that we would find the right treatment for her. It was right there in the NICU with JT when he reminded me about the ketogenic diet. I *declined* a trial of the diet. I felt so overwhelmed with our current situation, I could not imagine how I would implement such a strict and rigorous diet on a daily basis. I told him that we were not ready for that type of treatment; I was not able to understand how "food" could help her.

JT's doctors were able to successfully diagnose him with Hirschsprung's disease and alleviate the internal pressure by inserting rectal catheters three times daily. We were told we would have to continue this routine at home for at least the next four months until he was old enough to have a corrective surgery.

At this point Charlotte was having *thousands* of myoclonic seizures daily; sometimes they would come one after another making her not able to function at all. She had lost nearly all of her speech and all her beautiful blond, curly hair fell out after starting taking Depakote®. I spent the next four months taking care of JT and his three-times-a-day irrigations and calling Charlotte's neurologist's office several times a week due to uncontrollable seizures. Charlotte tried and failed phenobarbital, Trileptal®, Lamictal®, Depakote®, Topamax®, Gibatril®, Ativan®, Klonopin®, prednisone, and Stiripentol®. We were lost in a never-ending fog of seizures and Diastat®. Some days, the only thing Charlotte ate was her seizure medications. Our beautiful daughter was slipping away from us a little further each day.

On top of it all, we had to sell our house and move our family to Massachusetts to be closer to Steve's job at Hanscom AFB. The 26-mile commute to work had become too far for Steve what with all the emergency department and doctor visits. JT had his surgery—which was a total success—in June of 2007, and in March of 2008, we finally were able to sell our house and move on base at Hanscom. We were there for only four months before we found out that Steve was being transferred to a new assignment in Virginia.

When we arrived in Virginia, Charlotte began seeing Dr. Phillip Pearl at Children's National Medical Center. The first thing we did was put her on Clobazam®; she responded very well to this medication and was able to control most of her myoclonic seizures during the day. They would only come on strong right before her medication was due. We were happy with this control and Charlotte was doing well—this was such a welcome respite from all of the non-stop seizures of the previous 2 years. She started pre-school and her development took off. Her speech was still delayed, but she was happy.

In the spring of 2010 she suddenly lost seizure control and went downhill quickly. It seemed as though her medication just stopped working. We were back to the days of non-stop head drops that made her not able to function at all. I knew it was time to start the diet and, after meeting with Dr. Tammy Tsuchida and Laura Cramp, R.D., for evaluation, we were admitted to Children's National Medical Center to start the ketogenic diet. All began well and by the second day her myoclonic seizures were gone! We had not seen a day free from seizures since she was 18 months old! I was determined to make this diet work for her.

By the third day in the hospital, Charlotte was worn out and cranky. She took a nap and was not able to wake up. Her blood tests showed that her blood was too acidic. Charlotte was immediately put on regular doses of Bicitra® and given intravenous fluids to counteract the acid in her blood. Charlotte was able to wake up the following day and start eating again. After discovering that the meals she was eating were not accurately measured, Laura and I agreed that from then on, we could order meal ingredients and I would weigh and prepare the meals in our room. Our time in the hospital was doubled from three days to six, and it took weeks for Charlotte to fully regain her energy levels.

Grasping the concept that "food" can have such profound results for controlling seizures or making someone so ill is not easy. Feeding Charlotte 20 g (approximately 20 ml) of oil at each meal initially felt *wrong*; however, the absence of seizures resulting from the fat-filled meals was nothing short of a miracle. I had to re-train my brain to think about feeding and cooking for her in a whole new way.

Having Charlotte on the ketogenic diet started off with elation—the first day in over four years with no seizures—but it quickly turned into a frightening scenario when she developed acidosis. Once we were home I was consumed with stress trying to fit this new way of eating into our already busy lives. Ironically, I felt so stressed about preparing her meals that I was not able to even *enjoy* her new freedom from seizures. Slowly, the meal preparation became easier and I discovered a few tricks and methods that made life easier for all of us. Charlotte found new favorite meals and I started taking pictures. I put these pictures in a small photo album and allowed Charlotte to look at her food and pick out a meal or snack. We are now able to turn almost any recipe into a keto meal for Charlotte, and we often eat out in restaurants with Charlotte and her special meal! We have explained the diet to everyone in Charlotte's life, especially her teachers at school, and they all understand the importance of the diet's limitations. We have also prepared shelf-stable emergency snacks to keep at school and in the car in the event that our day does not go as planned.

We hope to continue the ketogenic diet for a very long time. Although she is not seizure free, we have nearly eliminated the daily myoclonics. There has not been any other medication or treatment that can even come close to the results of the diet. We continue to work very closely with Laura, our keto dietitian, and the rest of the keto team to fine tune the diet and adjust her medications for maximum results.

I have spent countless hours trying to make Charlotte's food as healthy and enjoyable as possible and it is our hope that we can help promote the diet as something that *anyone* can do if the ketogenic diet is indicated as a possible treatment. Currently, there are limited resources for recipes and meal preparation for ketogenic food, and we hope that the recipes in this book can be implemented into current keto diet plans and may even be able to help someone see that the diet *is* achievable, and food can still be enjoyable. Above all, it is my hope that another parent lost in the relentless fog of epilepsy can see pictures of ketogenic meals and understand the power that "food" can have, and be willing to give the diet a chance.

A DIETITIAN'S PERSPECTIVE

I first met Dawn, Steve, and Charlotte Martenz on May 20, 2010, in the ketogenic diet clinic at Children's National Medical Center. Charlotte, one of the most adorable little girls I have ever seen, was sitting quietly on the examination table. Her parents, like most parents I see in our clinic, appeared eager to learn more about the diet, but were scared that, yet again, another treatment would not work for their daughter. Having explained the diet hundreds of times, I went right into talking about fats and calories and what day-to-day life on the diet is really like. I mentioned a gram scale and "strict food measurements." I asked them about Charlotte's diet history and did she ever show any tendencies toward being a "picky eater." Looking back on this, I have to laugh at myself. Charlotte was a five-year-old girl and of course she had strong food preferences, and what did I know about the "strict food measurements"? I had never spent an entire month, week, or day making the recipes I was about to prescribe to Charlotte.

Thankfully, they were well informed about the diet. They came with a list of questions for me, such as "How soon will Charlotte be able to come off of her medications?" "How quickly will the diet start working?" and "What happens if Charlotte accidentally eats one of her brother's foods?" Due to the elusive mechanisms of the diet, most of these questions depend on how the individual child responds to the diet; there are no clear answers. The one question I could answer was "How soon can she be admitted to start the diet?"

One month later, Charlotte was admitted to the Neurology Unit at Children's National Medical Center to start the ketogenic diet. Having already obtained a food record from her parents, I began writing out menus for Charlotte to meet her calorie and ratio needs. I wrote things like *"mayonnaise and chicken breast: chop chicken and mix with mayonnaise to make chicken salad"* and *"egg, 40% cream and butter: mix egg with butter and cream and cook."* Charlotte reluctantly ate the food she was served, despite the egg swimming in butter and cream or the chicken smothered in so much mayonnaise it no longer resembled a chicken breast. Her parents were extremely patient with the process, but by the second day of her hospital admission Charlotte started to go downhill. She was sleeping a lot and vomiting; she refused to even sit up. She stopping drinking fluids and her parents had to force feed her to keep her blood sugar within a normal range. We checked her blood and saw that her serum bicarbonate level was dropping rapidly. She was developing metabolic acidosis, a common reaction when transitioning to the ketogenic diet. It took intravenous fluids and the administration of an alkaline agent, Bicitra®, to correct her blood levels and return Charlotte back to her baseline activity level. In the midst of all of this, her parents had brought in the scale they were to begin using after discharge and decided to measure the food as it was being brought to the room. It was a good thing they did, because as it turns out, the measurements were incorrect. The system I had in place for measuring the food in the kitchen was resulting in incorrect amounts of food being delivered.

My experience with Charlotte's diet initiation changed the way I approach initiation of the diet in our program. I know *now* that I really have no idea what day-to-day life is like for a family with a child on the ketogenic diet and that success on the diet can only be achieved through the collaboration of a knowledgable neurologist, a flexible dietitian, and most importantly, a dedicated parent/guardian. The parents are the people who will be working the hardest, planning, measuring, and cooking the meals. We have re-structured our keto program at Children's National with our goal to have the parents and guardians at the center of the meal preparation, using *their own* gram scale to measure the food, and cooking it *themselves* in the kitchen on the neurology unit while under the supervision of the keto team. Parent/caregiver education and training are equally important as actually initiating the diet.

Metabolic acidosis with vomiting and lethargy is not uncommon when starting the ketogenic diet, which is why we require all children to be admitted to the hospital to begin the diet. If Charlotte had not been in the hospital with close monitoring of her blood glucose and bicarbonate levels, the outcome could have been much worse.

After Charlotte's harrowing diet initiation, she was discharged to continue the diet at home. Although the diet has been successful at reducing her seizures, frequent communication is required between her mother, the neurology team, and me. I communicate with many parents and guardians of my patients on a weekly, if not daily, basis. Even in the most stable and well-controlled patient, the strict parameters of the diet need to be adjusted every few months to account for growth changes and to address any obstacles to diet success such as food refusal, constipation, and changes in seizure control. The number one rule I have for starting the ketogenic diet is: *You must come to your follow-up visits*! Without close monitoring of growth measurements and frequent communication about day-to-day issues, a ketogenic diet team will be ineffective at doing their job. This team approach is critical to success and without it the diet can be very dangerous.

One thing many families have in common prior to starting the diet is a sense of urgency to begin the initiation process. Never attempt to begin the diet at home without the supervision of a qualified team. Instead, at your initial consultation with the ketogenic diet team that will be following you, talk about what you can do to prepare for a smooth transition onto the diet. Have any current medications and supplements switched to sugar-free or low-carbohydrate versions. Locate appropriate sources for over-the-counter vitamins, fever reducers, and allergy medications that will be compatible with the diet. Change personal hygiene items to low-carbohydrate versions that are recommended by The Charlie Foundation.

Begin to keep a food journal and record daily the meals and snacks your child is eating. Keeping a detailed food journal can be a very valuable tool once the diet has begun. Finding correlations between foods, calorie level changes, ratio changes, and seizure activity will be much easier to identify if detailed records are kept. Depending upon your keto center, you may also be asked to track blood glucose and ketones.

If you are considering the diet, do not feed your child ketogenic meals just to "try them out." If a child hasn't eaten in a few hours, it can take as little as one ketogenic meal to induce ketosis. Instead, work with your keto team to try certain food items such as heavy cream, mayonnaise, butter, and oil as a part of a regular diet to test for your child's acceptance of these foods. Reduce the consumption of highly processed, high-carbohydrate foods and incorporate more whole foods such as fresh fruit, vegetables, and unprocessed protein. Initiate new rules at home such as eating only at the kitchen table and having meals and snacks at regular times. Avoid the habit of allowing kids to walk around the house with food and snacks that can easily be dropped or eaten by another child.

Making a few changes prior to starting the diet will reduce the overall stress for caregivers and help create a smoother transition onto the diet for everyone involved. Take advantage of this time; before you are busy preparing ketogenic meals, put these new habits and routines into practice.

Most importantly, this diet is not a "miracle" for everyone. It is just like any other anti-epileptic treatment; it must be prescribed by a medical professional and monitored closely. Not all children respond to the diet in the same way, so having the support and guidance of a medical team is essential.

Household and Community Hazards

B ecause the task of keto meal preparation is daunting enough for many families, the environment is often not taken into consideration as factor in success while on the diet.

Here are two pictures of a typical home kitchen. There is nothing extraordinary about it, but it is filled with potential keto hazards that could quickly derail the level of seizure control you may have achieved, or become a source for potential diet "cheating" unknown to the caregivers.

Can you identify the seventeen possible "hazards"?

See page 24 for answers.

1. _____   10. _____

2. _____   11. _____

3. _____   12. _____

4. _____   13. _____

5. _____   14. _____

6. _____   15. _____

7. _____   16. _____

8. _____   17. _____

9. _____

The pictures now identify each hazard with a number.

1. Baking ingredients in clear view, such as flours, sugars, oats, chocolate chips, etc. Beware of canisters on counter tops.
2. Pet food at ground level.
3. Purse hanging on chair, which often contains mints, gum, candies, lotions, and makeup.
4. Finished meal on table not cleared away, with crumbs, scraps of food, and unattended beverages.
5. High chair with food on the seat and on the floor, possibly left from a non-keto child.
6. House plants. Carbohydrates come in many forms and are not always in the form of food. This risk can depend on age and developmental level.
7. Paper napkins/paper towels. Wood pulp is a carbohydrate and could effect ketosis if ingested. Again, this can be related to age and developmental level.
8. Candy bowl or cough drops.

9. Sugar cup near a coffee pot.
10. Scented hand soap and lotion.
11. Fruit bowl.
12. Open pantry door, filled with favorite foods and snack items for other family members. Childproof locks are available.
13. Junk drawer, which may include candies, gum, lip balm, makeup, glue, lotions, etc.
14. Cookie jar.
15. Refrigerator/freezer within reach; childproof locks are available.
16. Vitamins and medications in reach; always keep out of reach and sight in childproof containers.
17. Cooking food, smells, and aromas may be too tempting even for older children to not sneak a bite.

As you can see, there are many areas where hidden carbohydrates can be found and eaten without a caregiver even realizing it has happened. While age and the developmental level of the keto patient is the first thing to consider, the overwhelming urge to obtain carbohydrates can be very intense. This is especially true during the beginning stages of the diet when the keto patient is adjusting to the new way of eating. Children who previously were never interested in the sugar bowl may find it to be a source for a sweet-tasting treat and consume sugar when no one is looking.

There is a behavioral disorder, pica, which is characterized by a desire to eat non-food items. It is most common in women and children. It is not caused by the ketogenic diet, but its trigger is not clearly defined, so keeping even non-food items out of reach may be important for some children, especially those with developmental disabilities. Chalk, soap, paper products, and even dirt are some items that are commonly ingested.

All environments where the keto patient spends time must be considered. This includes the family car, school, daycare center, homes of family and friends, and any other environment where your child will regularly spend time, especially when you are not present.

Many families are accustomed to sometimes eating in the car, and it will be worth the time and effort to thoroughly clean the car before starting the diet. A child would find it difficult to refrain from picking up an old raisin and eating it after starting the diet! Car seats and floor mats are filled with hiding places for discarded or dropped food, and you should prepare accordingly.

School environments often use paint, Play-Doh™, glue, and sensory tables filled with rice, beans, or oats. It may be possible for carbohydrates to be absorbed through the skin, which could affect ketosis in some patients. The school or daycare situation should be thoroughly discussed with school officials and parents.

This is not a complete list of keto hazards. Every home and environment is different and every keto patient has different needs, and this should be considered. Keeping the home environment as clean as possible and keeping food out of sight and locked away when necessary will lessen the temptation for the keto patient and reduce the stress on the caregiver. Informing all the people involved in your child's life about the special considerations associated with the diet should always be a top priority. If seizures remain an issue when the diet is followed as prescribed, analyze these potential pitfalls carefully as a source of cheating on the diet.

As the keto patient and the caregivers adjust to life on the diet, you may find that some of these areas may not be of concern in your own situation. Over time, keto patients become less sensitive to watching others eat "typical" foods or being in the presence of food that is not keto friendly. The intense urge to eat carbohydrate-loaded foods will slowly decrease, and newly formed keto habits and a new "normal" will settle in. Keep in mind that kids tend to be extremely resilient. While they may fight change, they tend to adapt to new routines better than adults. Often, parents feel that changing old habits or eliminating favorite foods is *never going to work*. This tends to be more of a problem for the caregiver than for the keto patient! Overcoming this mindset takes determination, strength, organization, and sometimes just a leap of faith. Even non-keto family members, especially siblings, will become aware of the importance of the diet's limitations and hopefully the potential reduction of seizures will prove to be a welcome trade-off for the lifestyle changes that have been made by everyone involved.

Conversion Chart for Easy Meal Assembly

U se this chart for easy meal assembly in emergency situations such as when you do not have access to a kitchen, or are eating out, or have misplaced your recipes.

Fat	Plus Protein	Plus Carbohydrate	Plus Cream	Equals 250–300 Calories of a 4:1 Ratio Meal
10 g mayonnaise	40 g scrambled eggs	12 g celery (raw)	48 g 36% cream	
10 g butter	16 g salmon (cooked)	7 g tomato (raw)		
8 g oil	16 g ground beef, 80% lean (cooked)	4 g broccoli (raw)		
	16 g canned tuna	4 g spinach (cooked)		
	13 g turkey breast (cooked)	3 g carrots (raw)		
	12 g pork tenderloin (cooked)	3 g strawberry		
	12 g fresh tuna (cooked)	3 g watermelon		
	12 g chicken breast (cooked)	2 g apple		
		2 g apple sauce		
		2 g orange		
		11 g cucumber		

Fat	Plus Protein	Plus Carbohydrate	Plus Cream	Equals 200–250 Calories of a 3:1 Ratio Meal
		4 g blackberries		
		3 g raspberries		
10 g mayonnaise	70 g scrambled eggs	12 g celery (raw)	40 g 36% cream	
10 g butter	23 g salmon (cooked)	7 g tomato (raw)		
8 g oil	25 g ground geef, 80% lean (cooked)	4 g broccoli (raw)		
	23 g canned tuna	4 g spinach (cooked)		
	20 g turkey breast (cooked)	3 g carrots (raw)		
	20 g pork tenderloin (cooked)	3 g strawberry		
	18 g fresh tuna (cooked)	3 g watermelon		
	17 g chicken breast (cooked)	2 g apple		
		2 g apple sauce		
		2 g orange		
		11 g cucumber		
		4 g blackberries		
		3 g raspberries		

Sample Letters

U se these letters to help notify flight attendants, airport security personnel, teachers, caregivers, and medical personnel of your child's special diet. It is helpful to keep a copy of the letter with you at all times for the emergency department, just in case you need to make a last-minute visit to the hospital. Most emergency departments are not familiar with how to manage a child on the ketogenic diet and will need guidance on what intravenous fluids and medications are safe.

LETTER TO THE TRANSPORTATION SECURITY ADMINISTRATION

To Whom It May Concern:

This letter is intended to inform the Transportation Security Administration of _(Insert Name)_'s special health care needs.

(Insert Name) has _(Insert Diagnosis)_ and is on a special diet to help control seizures. The ketogenic diet is an extremely precise high fat diet. _(Insert Name)_'s diet has been individually calculated by a dietitian and meals have to be weighed precisely on a gram scale.

(Insert Name)'s diet requires _(him/her)_ to consume food specifically calculated for _(him/her)_. _(Insert Name)_ will be traveling and will need to carry a supply of ketogenic food, beverages, and supplies. It is imperative that _(he/she)_ receives only the foods that have been weighed and prepared by _(his/her)_ caregivers.

In addition, _(he/she)_ will need to bring measuring utensils, a cooler, and a gram scale to measure all of _(his/her)_ food. _(He/She)_ may also need to monitor blood sugar or ketones while traveling, so _(he/she)_ will also need to carry a glucometer or ketone meter and lancets.

The ketogenic diet team at _(Insert Name of Medical Center/Hospital)_ appreciates your cooperation. If there are specific questions or concerns please contact _(Insert Name of Dietitian)_, pediatric dietitian, at _(Insert Phone Number of Dietitian)_ or Dr. _(Insert Name of Neurologist)_, at _(Insert Phone Number of Neurologist)_.

Sincerely,

Dr. _(Insert name of Neurologist)_
Pediatric Neurologist
(Insert Name of Medical Center/Hospital)

LETTER FOR SCHOOL/DAYCARE CENTER

To Whom It May Concern:

This letter is intended to inform any caretakers of *(Insert Name)* that *(he/she)* has been placed on a medical diet, the ketogenic diet.

The ketogenic diet is an extremely high fat, low-carbohydrate diet provided as a treatment for children with epilepsy and certain metabolic disorders. *(Insert Name)*'s diet has been individually calculated by a dietitian and meals have to be weighed precisely on a gram scale. *(Insert Name of Caregiver)* will be supplying these meals and snacks to you. Please give *(Insert Name)* *only* the meals and snacks from home and no other foods by mouth, as it could trigger a seizure. This also applies to beverages.

(Insert Name) is encouraged to drink *(Insert Fluid Amount)* ounces of *only* sugar-free, calorie-free beverages per day. *(Insert Name)*'s medications have also been changed to a sugar-free form to provide less carbohydrates.

The ketogenic diet team at *(Insert Name of Medical Center/Hospital)* appreciates your cooperation. If there are specific questions or concerns please contact *(Insert Name of Dietitian)*, pediatric dietitian, at *(Insert Phone Number of Dietitian)* or Dr. *(Insert Name of Neurologist)*, at *(Insert Phone Number of Neurologist)*.

Please notify *(Insert Name of Emergency Contact)* immediately if *(Insert Name)* has consumed any food, beverage or non-food item outside of the prescribed meals/snacks for the diet.

Sincerely,

Dr. *(Insert name of Neurologist)*
Pediatric Neurologist
(Insert Name of Medical Center/Hospital)

LETTER TO BRING TO HOSPITAL EMERGENCY DEPARTMENT OR PRIMARY PHYSICIAN

To Whom It May Concern:

This letter is intended to inform medical personnel of *(Insert Name)*'s special health care needs.

(Insert Name) has *(Insert Diagnosis)* and is on the ketogenic diet. The ketogenic diet is an extremely precise high fat diet. *(Insert Name)*'s diet has been individually calculated by a dietitian and meals have to be weighed precisely on a gram scale.

Please refrain from administering any dextrose-containing intravenous fluids or carbohydrate-containing medications. In may be helpful to add an allergy to dextrose on *(Insert Name)'s* chart or documentation, so that it is visible to food service, pharmacy, and nursing staff. *(Insert Name)* will need to maintain ketosis, with a goal of 4+ urine ketones, and should maintain a blood glucose level above 40 mg/dl. To treat a blood glucose below this range, please provide 15–30 ml juice and recheck after 15 minutes (Note that these values may be different for your specific ketogenic diet program).

The ketogenic diet team at *(Insert Name of Medical Center/Hospital)* appreciates your cooperation. If there are specific questions or concerns please contact *(Insert Name of Dietitian)*, pediatric dietitian, at *(Insert Phone Number of Dietitian)* or Dr. *(Insert Name of Neurologist)*, at *(Insert Phone Number of Neurologist)*. The on-call neurologist can also be reached at *(Insert on-call contact number)*.

Sincerely,

Dr. *(Insert name of Neurologist)*
Pediatric Neurologist
(Insert Name of Medical Center/Hospital)

Emergency Planning Guide

The day-to-day meal preparation of the ketogenic diet is hard enough to plan without the emergency situations that can arise that cause the diet to come to a screeching halt. Nothing can be scarier than the thought of not having the required medications, medical equipment, and specialized food available. Even having the primary caregiver temporarily unavailable may be problematic for some families. Here are some basic planning measures that can help you be ready for unexpected events.

PRIMARY CAREGIVER IS SUDDENLY UNAVAILABLE

Although many family and friends may surround a keto patient, usually one person bears the brunt of keto meal preparation, medicine administration, and additional therapies. Make it a priority to have more than one person responsible or trained to handle the daily routines and basic care. This includes access to the Ketocalculator (or other similar program); ability to cook a keto meal properly; realization of the importance of using the specific brands or types of food in keto meals; access to up-to-date medication/supplement doses and schedules; access to important contact information for doctors, pharmacies, dietitians, and therapists; and training on how to handle a seizure.

YOUR DAY DOES NOT GO AS PLANNED

Many days are filled with activities and running from one place to another. In many cities, it is easy to quickly become stuck in a traffic jam or have your plans changed at the last minute due to circumstances out of your control. Meal times can sneak up on you and suddenly, with home nowhere in sight, it is time to eat a meal or snack and there is no possible way to prepare one. Simply keep an extra shelf-stable meal and snack in your car, in a diaper bag, at your child's school or daycare center, or anywhere where your child spends time outside of the home. If you are traveling more than a few hours away from home, but expect to return home before the next meal, bring a meal with you anyway. And perhaps even bring your scale and think ahead to where you could purchase ingredients to create a meal. Be sure to have several basic meal plans and snacks that include easily obtained ingredients with you or your child at all times.

WEATHER EMERGENCIES, NATURAL DISASTERS, AND NATIONAL EMERGENCIES

In some areas, the first snowflake or a forecast of a hurricane can send masses of people running to the grocery store to purchase enough food to make it through the next several days. A natural disaster or national emergency can paralyze a city's infrastructure making it impossible to buy food, medications, or even have a clean water supply. The last thing you need to worry about is how you are going to find food to feed your keto child. Emergency planning is wise for all members of the family, with special consideration taken into account for a keto family member. Take the time to assemble a minimum of three days worth of food, water, clothing, medications, and personal care items for all members of your family. Keep an ample supply or buy in bulk those items that you cannot quickly and easily purchase, including MCT oils, ketogenic formulas such as KetoCal, and any specialized feeding equipment or supplies such as food thickeners, feeding bags, and syringes. Also, keep a supply of batteries for your gram scale, feeding pump, and any other equipment that may fail if the power is out.

An easy way to prepare for emergencies is to have a supply of shelf-stable food on hand. Simple items purchased in a grocery store ahead of time can make a huge difference in your level of preparedness. For each meal, you would need to have a fat, protein, and carbohydrate. Easy sources of protein include canned or pouch-style tuna, salmon, clams, and other seafood; canned or pouch-style chicken and beef (try to find brands with minimal added ingredients); plain unflavored nuts of all varieties; and powdered eggs and egg whites. Baby foods have varieties of plain proteins in a puree form that may be suitable for children with feeding difficulties.

Canned and bottled fruit and vegetables come in many different varieties; choose options that are canned or bottled in water or brands that specify "no added sugar." Good options for canned vegetables include green beans, spinach, squash, asparagus, mushrooms, and tomatoes. You could also use smaller amounts of corn, carrots, and peas. Again, the baby food aisle is an easy source for fruit and vegetables in small, pureed portions.

There are several great resources for shelf-stable foods. Many are specifically designed for emergency preparedness. You can find almost any protein, fruit, or vegetable in freeze-dried form. These foods do not contain any added ingredients or fillers, they just have the moisture removed to make them shelf stable in a sealed can or pouch. You can find a large selection at Emergency Essentials (www.beprepared.com). Be sure you purchase plain, single-ingredient foods—there are many varieties containing multiple ingredients designed to create an all-in-one meal, but these are not keto friendly. You will need water to prepare these foods, so the diet plans should be designed to weigh the ingredients in their dry state.

Make certain that whatever type of emergency food you keep on hand, that you also have the dietitian-approved meals plans to go along with it. The food will be of no use to you if you do not know how to properly prepare and incorporate it into a meal plan. Keep plenty of extra fat on hand, such as olive, coconut, and canola oils and canned coconut milk. Water is essential to everyone, and can easily be purchased in 16 oz., 2.5-, and 5-gallon containers. Keep all prescription medications filled and up-to-date, and have keto-friendly over-the-counter medications on hand at all times. A small amount of planning can go a long way in avoiding added stress and worry about special diets in emergency situations. The diet cannot safely be stopped abruptly, especially if it is effective at controlling seizures, so planning ahead to ensure continuation of the diet under any circumstance is essential.

BREAKFAST COOKIES *(p. 41)*   **EGG AND RED PEPPER BREAKFAST CUPS** *(p. 42)*

BERRY CALFLUTTI *(p. 44)*

BACON AND EGG CREAM CUPS *(p. 43)* ·   **PIGS IN A BLANKET** *(p. 45)*

FRUIT PIZZA *(p. 46)*

WARM FLAXMEAL CEREAL AND FRIED EGG WHITE *(p.*

MAPLE FLAVORED PORK BAKE *(p. 47)*

MICROWAVED BACON AND EGGS *(p. 49)*

CREAM-FILLED CREPES WITH STRAWBERRY PUREE *(p. 5*

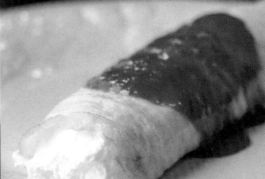

FRUIT SMOOTHIE AND BACON *(p. 51)*

CEREAL AND "MILK" *(p. 52)*

EGG AND SWISS CHARD SOUFFLE *(p. 55)*

PUMPKIN MICROWAVE PUDDING *(p. 53)*

CRANBERRY CRUMB CAKE *(p. 54)*

CINNAMON VANILLA EGG CUSTARD *(p. 56)* **SAVORY TURKEY HASH** *(p. 57)*

YOGURT PARFAIT *(p. 60)*

FRIED EGG WHITES AND HASH *(p. 58)* **PROTEIN WAFFLE** *(p. 59)*

CHICKEN NUGGETS *(p. 61)*   FLAX CRACKERS AND OLIVE TAPENADE *(p. 62)*

QUESADILLA WITH CREAMY AVOCADO DIP *(p. 66)*

EGG SALAD WITH CELERY ROOT CHIPS *(p. 64)*   CREAM OF CHICKEN SOUP *(p. 65)*

BROCCOLI CHEESE SOUP *(p. 67)*   **AVGOLEMONO (LEMON AND EGG SOUP)** *(p. 68)*

TURKEY AND CHEESE ROLL-UP'S *(p. 70)*

TUNA PATTIES *(p. 69)*   **TATER TOTS** *(p. 71)*

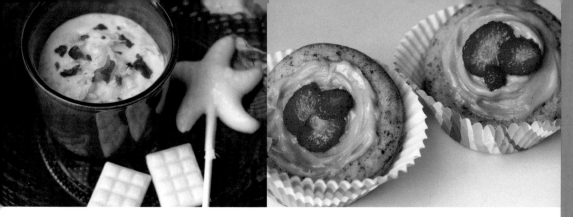

CLAM CHOWDER (p. 72)

PBJ COOKIES (p. 73)

SALMON SALAD (p. 76)

TUNA SALAD BOATS (p. 74)

FISH STICKS WITH TARTER SAUCE (p. 75)

FONDUE WITH VEGGIES *(p. 77)*   **CHICKEN SALAD SANDWICH WRAP** *(p. 78)*

RAINBOW TROUT ROLL-UPS *(p. 80)*

WHITE CHICKEN CHILI *(p. 79)*   **SIMPLE CHOPPED LUNCH** *(p. 81)*

BAKE AND FREEZE PIZZA *(p. 85)*   **MEATBALL CUP** *(p. 86)*

TACOS *(p. 83)*

KETO "HAMBURGER HELPER" *(p. 87)*   **POT ROAST** *(p. 88)*

BEEF AND SPAGHETTI SQUASH IN ALFREDO SAUCE *(p. 89)*　　　　**BEEF MOLE** *(p. 90)*

CHICKEN CURRY PATTIE *(p. 92)*

CARBONARA *(p. 91)*　　　　　　**BBQ PORK SHOULDER AND COLESLAW** *(p. 93)*

CRAB CAKES AND TARTAR SAUCE *(p. 95)*   **TERIYAKI SALMON CAKES** *(p. 96)*

SHRIMP CURRY *(p. 99)*

PORK STIR FRY WITH GINGER CREAM SODA *(p. 97)*   **SAUTÉED LAMB WITH POMEGRANATE, FETA, AND WALNUTS** *(p. 98)*

CABBAGE BOLOGNESE *(p. 100)*   **CHICKEN TETRAZZINI** *(p. 101)*

SUSHI *(p. 104)*

CHICKEN ENCHILADA CASSEROLE *(p. 102)*   **BROCCOLI, BACON, AND BLUE CHEESE MELT** *(p. 103)*

CINNAMON SUGAR PECANS *(p. 108)*

FRUIT TARTS *(p. 109)*

POP "UNDERS" *(p. 107)*

CHOCOLATE CUPCAKES *(p. 110)*

JELL-O® PUFFS *(p. 111)*

BRAZIL NUT COOKIES *(p. 112)*   NO-BAKE TROPICAL CREAM CHEESE BARS *(p. 113)*

NO-BAKE CHOCOLATE SNACK BARS *(p. 114)*

APPLES AND PEANUT BUTTER DIP *(p. 115)*   NO-COOK ALMOND BUTTER PUDDING *(p. 116)*

BASIC "SUGAR" COOKIES *(p. 117)*   **CHEESE CRACKERS** *(p. 118)*

VANILLA CUPCAKES *(p. 121)*

CHOCOLATE CUSTARD *(p. 119)*   **CHEESE-FILLED OLIVES** *(p. 120)*

FUDGE POPSICLE *(p. 122)*   **VEGGIES AND DIP** *(p. 123)*

CHOCOLATE-DIPPED "MARSHMALLOW" *(p. 125)*

PUMPKIN SEED MUFFINS *(p. 124)*   **HOMEMADE DAIRY-FREE YOGURT** *(p. 126)*

RECIPES

■ **BREAKFAST**

■ LUNCH

■ DINNER

■ SNACKS

CALORIES: 403
4:1 RATIO: 2 g CARBS

_____ 10 g European-style butter

_____ 9.7 g coconut oil

_____ 22 g pecans, ground

_____ 10 g sour cream

_____ 45 g raw egg, mixed well

_____ 3.5 g Truvia™, calorie-free sweetener

_____ 0.5 g cinnamon

_____ 0.1 g baking powder

_____ 3–5 drops of vanilla flavor, Bickford™

_____ pinch of salt

After measuring all ingredients on a gram scale, melt the butter and coconut oil together in a small mixing bowl. Add the remaining ingredients and stir well to combine. Divide the batter into silicone baking cups (about eight for this recipe) and bake in a 400°F oven for 15 minutes, until lightly browned on the edges.

Notes: Make in batches and freeze for up to 3 months. Thaw in the refrigerator, do not microwave.

Egg and Red Pepper Breakfast Cups

CALORIES: 409
4:1 RATIO: 2 g CARBS

_____ 7 g European-style butter

_____ 49 g raw egg, mixed well

_____ 20 g olive oil

_____ 15 g 40% heavy cream

_____ 8 g almond flour, Bob's Red Mill™

_____ 8 g diced red pepper, raw

_____ 0.1 g baking powder

Optional: salt/pepper

After measuring all ingredients on a gram scale, melt the butter in a small mixing bowl. Add the remaining ingredients and mix well. Divide batter into three silicone baking cups. Do not fill more than half way! Bake in a 350°F oven for about 15 minutes, until cooked thoroughly. Allow to cool in baking cups to reabsorb the fat.

Notes: If your child does not care for red pepper, ask your dietitian to modify the recipe to include a different vegetable such as spinach or broccoli.

Bacon and Egg Cream Cups

CALORIES: 407
4:1 RATIO: 1.5 g CARBS

_____ 7 g European-style butter

_____ 23 g pecans, ground

_____ 9.4 g bacon, Smithfield, no added sugar, cooked crisp

_____ 5 g olive oil

_____ 7 g egg whites, raw

_____ 12 g 40% heavy cream

_____ 7 g egg yolk, raw

_____ 4 g cheese, Kraft Cheddar, block style then grated

After measuring all ingredients on a gram scale, mince the cooked bacon into "crumb"-sized pieces. Melt the butter in a small mixing bowl. Add the pecans, bacon, olive oil, and egg white to the melted butter. Mix very well. Divide the mixture into three silicone baking cups and form them into "bowl" shapes. Mix the heavy cream and egg yolk together, pour into the center of the baking cups, and sprinkle the grated cheese on top. Bake in a 350°F oven for about 15 minutes until cooked thoroughly. Allow to cool in the baking cups to reabsorb the fat.

Berry Calflutti

CALORIES: 404
4:1 RATIO: 1.8 g CARBS

_____ 9 g European-style butter

_____ 34 g 40% heavy cream

_____ 60 g raw egg, mixed well

_____ 13 g walnut oil

_____ 1.6 g Truvia™, calorie-free sweetener

_____ 8 g fresh blackberries, sliced

After measuring all ingredients on a gram scale, preheat oven
to 350°F. In a wide, shallow tart dish, melt the butter in the
microwave. Coat the dish with the butter. Mix the cream, egg,
walnut oil, sweetener, and vanilla very well. Pour the mixture into
the dish; do not fill more than one-third full, as the egg mixture
will puff in the oven and you do not want the ingredients to
overflow. Place the blackberry pieces on top of the egg mixture.
Bake for about 15 minutes until cooked thoroughly. Let the calflutti
cool for a few minutes and serve warm.

Pigs in a Blanket

CALORIES: 405
4:1 RATIO: 1.9 g CARBS

Reminiscent of a diner breakfast! All the familiar flavors rolled into one—eggs, sausage, maple, and butter—and cooked quickly in a skillet.

_____ 36 g raw egg, mixed well

_____ 30 g 40% heavy cream

_____ 13.5 g mayonnaise, Hellman's™

_____ 12 g whole milk ricotta cheese

_____ 0.2 g baking powder

_____ 10 g European-style butter

_____ 13 g pork sausage links, Bob Evans Original, cooked

_____ 3–5 drops of maple flavor, Bickford™

Optional: salt, calorie-free sweetener

After measuring all ingredients on a gram scale, mix the egg, cream, mayonnaise, ricotta, baking powder, maple flavor, and optional ingredients together very well. Melt the butter in an 8- to 10-inch nonstick skillet on medium-low heat. Pour the batter into the skillet and let it spread into a very thin pancake. Cook the batter until the center has started to firm. Carefully flip to cook the other side. Cut the sausage links in half lengthwise and place in the center of the cooked batter. Roll the "blanket" around the sausage links. Scrape all of the remaining fat out of the pan onto the meal.

Fruit Pizza

CALORIES: 406
4:1 RATIO: 2.1 g CARBS

This is a very fun special-event or weekend meal. Pizza in the morning is an unexpected treat that makes kids happy!

_____ 39 g egg whites, raw, beaten stiff
_____ 18 g egg yolk, raw
_____ 17 g canola oil
_____ 3.5 g calorie-free sweetener, Truvia™
_____ 20 g 40% heavy cream, whipped
_____ 10 g European-style butter
_____ 6 g cream cheese, Philadelphia brand
_____ 7 g strawberries, minced
_____ 5 g blackberries, minced
_____ 3–5 drops of vanilla flavor, Bickford™

After measuring all ingredients on a gram scale, preheat the oven to 350°F. Fold the egg yolk, walnut oil, and half of the Truvia™ into the egg whites. Pour onto a lightly greased silicone- or parchment-lined baking sheet. Bake for 20–25 minutes until cooked thoroughly. While the crust is cooking, mix the cream cheese, butter, and vanilla until it is very smooth. Fold the remaining Truvia™ and whipped cream into the cream cheese mixture.

Assemble the pizza by spreading the cream cheese mixture onto the cooked crust. Make sure the bowl is scraped very well. Then evenly spread the chopped fruit on top.

Notes: The "crust" will hold all of the oil, but if a lighter and fluffier texture is preferred, serve some of the oil on the side.

Maple-Flavored Pork Bake

CALORIES: 405
4:1 RATIO: 1.9 g CARBS

Sweet and savory flavors blend together well in a mini-casserole style dish served with a side of vanilla ice cream.

_____ 40 g 40% heavy cream, whipped
_____ 3–5 drops of vanilla flavor, Bickford™
_____ 18.5 g ground pork, cooked
_____ 14 g macadamia nuts, crushed
_____ 11 g European-style butter
_____ 5 g cheese, Kraft Cheddar, block style, then grated
_____ 2 g calorie-free sweetener, Truvia™
_____ 3–5 drops of maple flavor, Bickford™

Optional: salt/pepper

After measuring all ingredients on a gram scale, mix the whipped cream with the vanilla flavor and half of the allotted Truvia™. Freeze for 15 minutes.

Preheat the oven to 350°F. In an oven-safe dish, mix the pork, macadamia nuts, butter, cheese, remaining Truvia™, maple flavor, and optional salt/pepper. Bake for 15 minutes to warm the ingredients through.

Serve with the frozen whipped cream as "ice cream."

Warm Flaxmeal Cereal and Fried Egg White

CALORIES: 404
4:1 RATIO: 1.8 g CARBS

If you are having trouble getting enough fiber while on the ketogenic diet, this warming cereal is the way to go! This is served with an egg white; you could also add fruit for a lower ratio. This recipe makes a large serving of cereal.

_____ 21 g flaxseed meal, Bob's Red Mill™
_____ 10 g European-style butter
_____ 5 g coconut oil
_____ 3–5 drops of vanilla flavor, Bickford™

_____ 45 g 40% heavy cream
_____ 33 g egg white, raw
_____ 0.1 g cinnamon
_____ pinch of salt

Measure the cream, flaxseed meal, and butter in a microwavable bowl. Microwave in 30-second intervals, stirring very well each time. The cereal only needs to be warmed through to thicken. It can be made very thick, similar in consistency to oatmeal; more water can be added to thin it to desired consistency. Add the cinnamon, vanilla flavor, and salt; stir to combine.

Melt the coconut oil in a small nonstick frying pan over medium-low heat. Fry the egg white in the coconut oil until cooked through. Place the egg white on a serving plate and scrape all of the remaining fat out of the pan onto the egg white.

Dietitian's Corner: Flax seeds contain large amounts of polyunsaturated fatty acids, which help lower blood cholesterol levels.

Eating excessive amounts of flax seeds or flax seed oil can lead to thinning of the blood. We do not recommend that you consume this recipe on a daily basis and to have your blood tested by your physician if you are consuming these products frequently and in large amounts.

CALORIES: 403
4:1 RATIO: 1 g CARBS

Precooked bacon helps this one-dish breakfast come together super fast for a busy morning.

_____ 45 g raw egg, mixed well

_____ 25 g 40% heavy cream

_____ 15 g European-style butter

_____ 9 g canola oil

_____ 8 g bacon, Smithfield brand, no added sugar, cooked

_____ salt/pepper

After measuring all ingredients on a gram scale, mix the eggs, cream, oil, and salt/pepper together very well in a 16-oz microwave-safe bowl. Add the butter and bacon—broken into smaller pieces—to the egg mixture. Microwave for about 1 minute or until thoroughly cooked. The eggs will puff up, and then deflate. Serve immediately in the same dish.

Cream-Filled Crepes with Strawberry Puree

CALORIES: 406
4:1 RATIO: 2.1 g CARBS

Sometimes, a change in presentation is all it takes to serve the same old ingredients. This is actually just an egg cooked in a very thin circle filled with whipped cream, but looks entirely different than scrambled eggs with strawberries and cream.

_____ 56.5 g raw egg, mixed well
_____ 44 g 40% heavy cream, whipped
_____ 10 g coconut oil, melted
_____ 9 g European-style butter
_____ 8 g strawberries, pureed or smashed with a fork
_____ 2 g calorie-free sweetener, Truvia™

Optional: 3–5 drops of vanilla flavor, Bickford™

After measuring all ingredients on a gram scale, melt the butter in an 8- to 10-inch nonstick skillet over medium heat. Mix the eggs with the coconut oil very well and pour into the pan. Cook for about 1 minute or until the edges are set and the center begins to firm up. Carefully flip to cook the other side. Move the crepe to a plate and scrape the remaining fat out of the pan onto the crepe. Mix the Truvia™ and vanilla flavor into the whipped cream and fill the center of the crepe. Roll up the crepe and spoon the strawberry puree on the top.

Notes: Omit the strawberries and replace with cocoa powder that has been mixed into the whipped cream for a chocolate flavor version.

Fruit Smoothie and Bacon

CALORIES: 408
4.01:1 RATIO: 2.2 g CARBS

Smoothies taste great and hide oil very well. There is also the added benefit of the smoothie "bulking up" the size of the meal. If you prefer not to serve bacon, an egg would be a great alternative.

_____ 49 g 40% heavy cream

_____ 75 g almond milk, Blue Diamond brand, unsweetened vanilla flavor

_____ 10 g walnut oil

_____ 5 g frozen blueberries, unsweetened

_____ 2 g calorie-free sweetener, Truvia™

_____ 18.5 g bacon, Smithfield brand, no sugar added, cooked

After measuring all ingredients on a gram scale, combine the heavy cream, almond milk, walnut oil, blueberries, and Truvia™ in a small blender cup and process until the blueberries are completely pureed. Scrape the blender blades very well and serve in the same cup along with the cooked bacon.

Notes: Use any type of unsweetened frozen fruit or fresh fruit.

Magic Bullet™-style blenders work the best for small smoothies because you can use the blender cup to drink from, minimizing food loss that happens with a larger blender. An immersion blender will also work well.

Cereal and "Milk"

CALORIES: 404
4:1 RATIO: 2.6 g CARBS

Breakfast cereal is often one of the foods that kids miss the most after starting the diet. This cereal may not be practical for an everyday meal, but makes a great treat for a weekend or birthday meal.

_____ 41 g egg whites, whipped into stiff peaks
_____ 14 g macadamia nuts, chopped
_____ 7 g coconut oil, melted
_____ 1.5 g Jell-O® powder, sugar free
_____ 1 g calorie-free sweetener, Truvia™
_____ 57 g 40% heavy cream

Preheat the oven to 325°F. After measuring all ingredients on a gram scale, carefully fold the macadamia nuts, coconut oil, Jell-O® powder, and Truvia™ into the egg whites. Mix until the color from the Jell-O® is evenly distributed. Spoon the mixture into a plastic sandwich baggie. Twist the top of the baggie closed and cut off about a 1/4 inch of the corner. Pipe "dime-sized" mounds of the egg white mixture onto a lightly greased parchment- or silicone-lined baking sheet. Make sure you squeeze all of the mixture out of the baggie. Bake for about 20–30 minutes or until the egg whites are dried out completely. Weigh the cream in a cereal bowl and add enough water to thin to desired consistency. Pour in the cooked "cereal" and serve immediately.

Notes: This makes a very large serving.

Store the cooked "cereal" in an air-tight container in the refrigerator until it is ready to be eaten.

Pumpkin Microwave Pudding

CALORIES: 406
4:1 RATIO: 2.2 g CARBS

This is so quick and easy to throw together on a busy morning. Tastes like warm pumpkin pie filling with a creamy texture similar to ricotta cheese.

_____ 30 g 40% heavy cream
_____ 36 g raw egg, mixed well
_____ 25 g ricotta cheese, whole milk
_____ 12 g walnut oil
_____ 11.7 g European-style butter
_____ 5 g canned pumpkin, unsweetened
_____ 2 g calorie-free sweetener, Truvia™
_____ 0.2 g cinnamon

Optional: pinch of salt, 3–5 drops of vanilla flavor, Bickford™

After measuring all ingredients on a gram scale, combine in a microwavable bowl. Heat in 30-second increments, stirring very well after each cycle. Heat the pudding until the temperature reaches 160°F. The eggs will begin to cook around the edges. Stir very well again and serve.

Notes: There is a very small amount of pumpkin puree in this recipe. For lower ratios, add more pumpkin!

Cranberry Crumb Cake

CALORIES: 408
4:1 RATIO: 2.2 g CARBS

You would never know that there is not even 1 gram of flour in this delicious cake. It is also packed with protein, so it is a great way to start your day!

_____ 23 g raw egg whites, whipped into stiff peaks
_____ 23 g raw egg yolks
_____ 11 g macadamia nuts, ground into butter
_____ 10 g coconut oil, melted
_____ 5 g fresh cranberries, chopped small
_____ 2 g calorie-free sweetener, Truvia™
_____ 0.3 g baking powder
_____ 0.1 g cinnamon
_____ 11 g pecans, ground fine
_____ 10.5 g European-style butter

Optional: pinch of salt, 3–5 drops of vanilla flavor, Bickford™

Preheat oven to 350°F. After measuring all ingredients on a gram scale, fold the egg yolks, macadamia nuts, coconut oil, cranberries, Truvia™, baking powder, cinnamon, and optional salt and vanilla flavor into the egg whites. Pour the batter into a lightly greased baking dish (about 2-cups capacity). Bake for about 15 minutes then spread the ground pecans and butter on the top of the cake. Continue baking until cooked thoroughly, about 20–25 minutes total.

Egg and Swiss Chard Souffle

CALORIES: 401
4:1 RATIO: 1.9 g CARBS

A great way to change up the same old breakfast routine! Bake this the night before and quickly warm it up in the microwave. This is a great combination of savory flavors.

———— 45 g raw egg whites, whipped into stiff peaks
———— 25 g 40% heavy cream
———— 24 g Swiss chard, raw, chopped fine
———— 14 g olive oil
———— 12 g egg yolk, raw
———— 2 g Dijon mustard, Grey Poupon brand
———— 15 g European-style butter

Optional: salt/pepper, garlic powder

Preheat the oven to 350°F. After measuring all ingredients on a gram scale, fold the cream, Swiss chard, olive oil, egg yolk, mustard, and optional seasonings into the egg whites. Place the butter in a 16-oz ramekin, and melt in the microwave. Swirl the melted butter around in the ramekin to cover the bottom and sides. Pour the egg white mixture into the ramekin and bake for about 25 minutes or until cooked thoroughly.

Cinnamon Vanilla Egg Custard

CALORIES: 404
4:1 RATIO: 1.8 g CARBS

Rich, creamy, and smooth, this can be enjoyed by anyone, and a smaller portion would be a great dessert!

_____ 58 g raw egg, mixed well
_____ 50 g 40% heavy cream
_____ 17 g European-style butter, melted
_____ 0.2 g cinnamon

Optional: Truvia™, 3–5 drops of vanilla flavor, Bickford™, pinch of salt

Preheat the oven to 350°F. Bring a kettle of water to a boil. After measuring all ingredients on a gram scale, combine and mix very well. Lightly grease a 16-oz ramekin and pour in the egg mixture. Place the ramekin in a larger casserole dish and fill the casserole dish with the boiling water. Make sure the water comes about half way up the sides of the ramekin. Bake for about 45 minutes or until the center of the custard is firm.

Notes: This can be made in a large batch. Weigh the butter separately from the egg mixture, right in the ramekins.

Savory Turkey Hash

CALORIES: 406
4:1 RATIO: 2.1 g CARBS

Not in the mood for eggs? This is the breakfast for you!

_____ 31.5 g turkey breast, Applegate Farms brand, roasted, torn into bite-sized pieces
_____ 25 g pecans, ground fine
_____ 16 g green bell peppers, chopped small
_____ 15 g European-style butter
_____ 10 g coconut oil
_____ pinch of dried sage

Optional: salt/pepper

Measure all ingredients on a gram scale. Melt the butter and coconut oil in a nonstick skillet. Add the remaining ingredients and fry over medium-low heat until slightly brown and crispy.

Notes: Swap out the turkey for another meat such as ham, ground beef or even tofu. Just ask your dietitian to recalculate.

Fried Egg Whites and Hash

CALORIES: 409
4.02:1 RATIO: 2.2 g CARBS

This is a very tasty breakfast! The cheese completely disguises the taste of the turnips and becomes an extra layer of crunchy goodness!

_____ 33 g egg whites, raw
_____ 15 g European-style butter
_____ 18 g turnips, raw, shredded
_____ 14 g cheddar cheese, Organic Valley brand, raw sharp cheddar, shredded
_____ 3 g scallions, raw, tops and bulbs, sliced thin
_____ 36 g 40% heavy cream
_____ 9 g walnut oil

Optional: salt/pepper, 3–5 drops of vanilla flavor, Bickford™

Measure all ingredients on a gram scale. Melt the butter in a nonstick frying pan. Add the egg whites and fry them until they are cooked thoroughly. Remove the cooked egg white to a serving plate. In the same pan, add the turnips and scallions. Fry until the turnips are tender and most of the moisture has cooked out. Sprinkle the cheese over the turnips and allow to become slightly brown and crisp. When the cheese stops bubbling, remove from the pan onto the serving plate. Scrape the pan to remove all of the fat onto the serving plate. Serve with the cream and oil mixed together as a milk drink or whip the cream and blend in the oil and optional flavoring for a pudding-type dessert.

Protein Waffle

CALORIES: 404
4:1 RATIO: 2.1 g CARBS

The protein waffle is based on the Charlie Foundation Macadamia Nut Waffle recipe. Instead of using ground macadamia nuts for the batter, ground pecans are used, giving the waffle a slightly different flavor.

_____ 39 g raw egg, mixed well
_____ 30 g pecans, ground fine
_____ 18 g 40% heavy cream
_____ 8 g coconut oil, melted
_____ 0.2 g baking powder

Optional: pinch of salt, 3–5 drops of vanilla flavor, Bickford™, pinch of cinnamon

Preheat an electric waffle iron. After measuring in a gram scale, mix all of the ingredients very well. Lightly spray the top and bottom of the waffle iron with spray oil. Pour the batter into the center of the iron and quickly close the waffle iron top, making sure not to overfill the waffle iron. If batter is lost out of the sides, you will have reduced the number of calories in the meal. Cook the waffle for about 1–3 minutes depending upon your waffle iron. The waffle should easily release from the iron when it has finished cooking. Carefully lift the waffle out and serve.

Yogurt Parfait

CALORIES: 403
4:1 RATIO: 4 g CARBS

*This recipe does not contain the recommended amount of protein,
so use sparingly or for a special treat if seizures are well controlled.*

_____ 1 serving of dairy-free keto yogurt (see Snack recipes)
_____ 20 g macadamia nuts, crushed
_____ 15.8 g kiwi fruit, chopped small
_____ 4 g flaxseed meal, Bob's Red Mill™
_____ 20 g 40% heavy cream, whipped

Optional: 3–5 drops of vanilla flavor, Bickford™

Empty the keto yogurt out of the container into a bowl. Make
sure you scrape the yogurt container very well. Top with the
macadamia nuts, kiwi fruit, flaxseed meal, and whipped cream
flavored with the vanilla if desired.

Chicken Nuggets

CALORIES: 406
4:1 RATIO: 1.6 g CARBS

Keto chicken nuggets look so much like real ones, and they will quickly become a favorite!

_____ 22 g egg whites, whipped into stiff peaks

_____ 2.5 g coconut flour, Bob's Red Mill™

_____ 12 g European-style butter

_____ 17 g chicken breast, cooked, shredded

_____ 0.5 g baking powder

_____ 20 g olive oil

_____ 23 g 40% heavy cream

Optional: salt, pepper, pinch of garlic powder

After measuring all ingredients on a gram scale, shred the chicken into very small pieces. Add the coconut flour, baking powder, and optional salt, pepper, and garlic powder to the shredded chicken. Stir to coat the chicken. The mixture should look very dry. Add the oil to the chicken mixture and mix again. Add the egg whites to the chicken and fold in until combined. Melt the butter in a small nonstick frying pan. Drop the chicken and egg mixture on the pan in small nugget-sized shapes and fry for about 1 minute. Flip to fry the other side until cooked thoroughly, for about 1 minute. Remove the cooked nuggets and place them on a plate and scrape any remaining butter out of the pan onto the nuggets. Serve with cream diluted with water as "milk."

Notes: If ratio allows, add fresh fruit such as strawberries that have been blended into a puree and mix into the cream to make a strawberry milk shake.

Ask for new empty containers at fast food restaurants to serve the chicken nuggets and milkshakes.

Ask your dietitian if you would like to add a dipping sauce such as low-sugar ketchup or mustard.

You can easily substitute any other cooked protein such as salmon or chicken livers.

Flax Crackers and Olive Tapenade

CALORIES: 405
4:1 RATIO: 1.5 g CARBS

Crispy crackers and a salty, savory dip! Blend the dip with an immersion blender for a smoother consistency.

For the crackers:

_____ 20 g flaxseed meal, Bob's Red Mill™
_____ 10 g parmesan cheese, block style, grated
_____ 9 g raw egg, mixed well
_____ 1 g calorie-free sweetener, Truvia™
_____ approximately 5 g water

Optional: salt/pepper, pinch of garlic powder

For the olive tapenade:

_____ 23 g mayonnaise, Hellman's™
_____ 6.2 g olive oil
_____ 15 g black olives, bottled, minced
_____ 15 g green olives, bottled, minced

Preheat the oven to 300°F. After measuring all ingredients on a gram scale, mix all of the cracker ingredients together and add water until the dough forms a ball. Place the dough between two sheets of parchment paper that have been lightly oiled. Roll the dough as thin as possible, about 1/8 inch. Remove the top piece of parchment and score the dough with a knife by pressing down, (do not drag) into cracker shapes. Transfer the rolled dough, keeping it on the parchment, to a baking sheet. Bake for about 30 minutes until the crackers have dried completely. Let them cool on the baking sheet and then break apart into the crackers.

Flax Crackers and Olive Tapenade (*Continued*)

Mix together the mayonnaise and olive oil. Using an electric hand mixer will prevent the oil from separating. Add the minced olives and mix well.

Dietitian's Corner: Flax seed contains a phytochemical called lignan, which has been theorized to reduce the risk of some cancers. The human body cannot break down the hard, fibrous shell of a flax seed, so it is best consumed in the ground form.

Egg Salad with Celery Root Chips

CALORIES: 407
4:1 RATIO: 1.9 g CARBS

Celery root is not a common vegetable to cook with, but it has a very mild flavor and can be cooked in a variety of ways, including baking into crispy chips!

_____ 10 g celery root, raw
_____ 19.5 g egg yolk, cooked
_____ 13.5 g olive oil
_____ 42 g egg white, cooked
_____ 25 g 40% heavy cream, whipped
_____ 14 g mayonnaise, Hellman's™

Optional: salt/pepper

Preheat the oven to 300°F. Slice the celery root paper thin, and then measure on a gram scale. Spread slices in a single layer on a parchment- or silicone-lined baking sheet. Do not overlap! Bake for about 30 minutes or until the chips are thoroughly crisp. After measuring all other ingredients on a gram scale, using an electric hand mixer, beat the egg yolks and oil until smooth. Season with salt and pepper. Fold in the chopped egg whites, whipped cream, and mayonnaise.

Notes: Hard boil eggs the night before.

Use a mandolin to slice the celery root.

Ask your dietitian to add in iceberg lettuce to wrap the egg salad, like a tortilla, if your child prefers.

Cream of Chicken Soup

CALORIES: 402
4:1 RATIO: 1.7 g CARBS

Chicken soup is always a favorite; adding the cream to make a keto version only adds to the comforting properties of the soup!

_____ 50 g 40% heavy cream
_____ 51 g chicken broth, Imagine free range
_____ 23 g chicken breast, cooked, diced small
_____ 10 g celery, sliced thin
_____ 10 g European-style butter
_____ 11 g coconut oil

Optional: salt/pepper

After measuring all ingredients on a gram scale, combine the cream, chicken broth, chicken breast, celery, and butter in a small microwave-safe bowl. Heat in 30-second intervals stirring each time until warmed through and celery has softened, about two and a half minutes total.

Notes: You can serve this "chunky" like the recipe above indicates, or you can puree this soup with an immersion blender for a very smooth consistency. Use xanthan gum for a thicker consistency.

Quesadilla with Creamy Avocado Dip

CALORIES: 404
4:1 RATIO: 1.9 g CARBS

A very tasty tortilla can be made out of egg whites and almond flour! This will not have the same texture as bread, but the cheese and avocado dip bring this meal together.

_____ 20 g 40% heavy cream
_____ 11 g mayonnaise, Hellman's™
_____ 5 g olive oil
_____ 23 g hass avocado
_____ 10 g European-style butter
_____ 30 g egg whites
_____ 5 g almond flour, Bob's Red Mill™
_____ 12 g cheese, Kraft Cheddar, block style, grated

Optional: salt/pepper, pinch of garlic powder or cayenne pepper

Measure all ingredients on a gram scale. In a small mixing bowl, combine the cream, mayonnaise, olive oil, and avocado. Blend until smooth with a hand mixer or use a fork to mash together for a chunkier consistency. Mix in the optional ingredients, if using. Mix the egg whites and almond flour together very well. Melt the butter in a small nonstick frying pan on medium heat. Pour the egg white mixture into the pan in a very thin layer. Cook until the egg is opaque, and then carefully flip to cook the other side. Let the edges brown and crisp slightly. Turn the heat off and sprinkle the cheese on top. Fold in half to melt the cheese. Remove the eggs from the pan and slice into wedges, scrape the remaining fat out of the pan onto the eggs, and serve with the avocado dip.

Dietitian's Corner: Avocado is the perfect keto food. It has naturally a 4:1 ratio, and it has full of heart-healthy fats. Avocados are made up of large amounts of monounsaturated fatty acids, which lower blood cholesterol. Avocado is also high in fiber, making them a natural treatment for constipation.

Broccoli Cheese Soup

CALORIES: 401
4:1 RATIO: 1.8 g CARBS

A quick and easy lunch that can be heated in the microwave!

———— 45 g chicken broth, Imagine free range
———— 42 g 40% heavy cream
———— 28 g cheese, Kraft Cheddar, block style, grated
———— 10 g coconut oil
———— 9 g broccoli, cooked
———— 5 g European-style butter

Optional: salt/pepper

Measure all ingredients on a gram scale. Put all of the ingredients in a microwave-safe bowl and heat in 30-second intervals until warmed through.

Notes: Leave the coconut oil out of the soup and serve as a frozen coconut candy.

Puree the soup with an immersion blender for a very smooth consistency.

Avgolemono (Lemon and Egg Soup)

CALORIES: 407
4:1 RATIO: 2.2 g CARBS

Avgolemeno is a Greek soup that traditionally includes chicken and orzo. The meat and starch are omitted in this version and create a smooth soup that is drinkable, if desired. This is a bright, clean-tasting soup thanks to the fresh lemon juice.

_____ 54 g raw egg, mixed well
_____ 52 g 40% heavy cream
_____ 50 g chicken broth, Imagine free range
_____ 16.8 g European-style butter
_____ 2 g fresh lemon juice

Optional: salt/pepper

After measuring all ingredients on a gram scale, combine the eggs, cream, broth, and butter in a microwavable bowl. Heat in 30-second increments, stirring well each time. The eggs need to be heated until they reach at least 160°F, or about 2 minutes total. The longer the soup is cooked, the thicker and more "scrambled" the eggs will become. When the soup has reached the desired consistency, stir in the lemon juice.

Notes: If the eggs have overcooked, use an immersion blender to bring it back to a smooth consistency.

Tuna Patties

CALORIES: 404
4.01:1 RATIO: 1 g CARBS

Tuna patties take on a kid-friendly "deep fried" flavor due to the coconut oil. They are best served at room temperature or straight from the refrigerator; this helps to disguise the fat and make them a finger food.

_____ 25 g canned tuna, Bumblebee chunk light in water, drained

_____ 2 g raw egg, mixed well

_____ 15 g mayonnaise, Hellmann's™

_____ 8 g almond flour, Bob's Red Mill™

_____ 11.5 g walnut oil

_____ 12 g coconut oil

Optional: salt/pepper

Weigh all ingredients on a gram scale. Mix the tuna, egg, mayonnaise, almond flour, walnut oil, and salt/pepper in a small bowl. Melt the coconut oil in a small nonstick skillet on medium heat. Make three patty shapes with the tuna and fry for 2–3 minutes. Flip to fry the other side until cooked thoroughly. A crunchier exterior will develop the longer they are cooked. Remove the cooked patties from the pan and scrape all of the remaining fat onto the patties. Store them in the refrigerator.

Notes: This recipe can be mixed in a large batch. Cook each serving separately.

Turkey and Cheese Roll-ups

CALORIES: 406
4:1 RATIO 1.8 g CARBS

This is like a turkey sandwich without the bread! The little bit of mustard added to the mayonnaise makes a tasty dip to pack along in a school lunch.

_____ 22 g turkey breast, Applegate Farms roasted

_____ 14 g cheddar cheese, Organic Valley, Raw Sharp Cheddar

_____ 6 g butterhead lettuce

_____ 26 g mayonnaise, Hellman's™

_____ 3 g yellow mustard

_____ 37 g 40% heavy cream

Weigh the turkey, cheese, and lettuce on a gram scale. Roll them up lengthwise and skewer with a fun toothpick if desired. Mix the mayonnaise and mustard together and serve as a dip. Serve the cream as a "milk" drink.

Notes: Ask the deli to slice a ½-inch thick slice of turkey. At home, dice this into small bite-sized squares. Replace the lettuce with diced cucumber and add the cheese cut into the same size for an easy dippable finger food–style meal.

Tater Tots

CALORIES: 405
4.01:1 RATIO: 2 g CARBS

Although these are not tater tots from the frozen food isle, they have a very similar taste and texture from the shredded turnips. This is also an all-in-one meal, so it is easy to eat at school or in the car.

_____ 46 g raw egg whites, whipped into stiff peaks
_____ 26 g mayonnaise, Hellman's™
_____ 21 g raw turnip, shredded
_____ 12.3 g walnut oil
_____ 8 g pecans, ground fine
_____ 6 g parmesan cheese, block style, shredded

Optional: salt/pepper, pinch of garlic powder

Preheat the oven 350°F. After measuring all ingredients on a gram scale, combine and mix well. Drop teaspoon-sized mounds onto a silicone- or parchment-lined baking sheet. Bake for about 20–25 minutes until they are cooked thoroughly.

Notes: You could use the allotted mayonnaise for a dipping sauce instead of cooking it into the meal or ask your dietitian if you would like to add a dipping sauce such as low-sugar ketchup or mayonnaise.

71

Clam Chowder

CALORIES: 407
4:1 RATIO: 2.2 g CARBS

Xanthan gum is the secret ingredient in this soup; 1/4 teaspoon added into the cream and broth makes the soup so thick and delicious, and you would never know it is not authentic "chowda." This is also served with coconut oil candy for a fun way to eat the extra fat.

_____ 35 g 40% heavy cream
_____ 50 g chicken broth, Imagine free range
_____ 18 g fresh clams, steamed
_____ 9.5 g European-style butter
_____ 9 g celery, raw, sliced thin
_____ 6.8 g bacon, Smithfield, no sugar added, cooked
_____ 1/4 teaspoon Xanthan gum, add more for a thicker soup
_____ 15 g coconut oil mixed with 1–2 drops of Bickford™ flavor, 1–2 drops
liquid sweetener then frozen to make coconut oil candy.

Optional: salt/pepper, garlic powder

After measuring all ingredients on a gram scale, mix the heavy cream, chicken broth, clams, butter, celery, and xanthan gum together in a microwavable bowl. Microwave in 30-second intervals, stirring very well each time, until heated to desired temperature. Add the bacon and the optional seasonings. Be careful not to over-salt, as the clams may add enough salt flavor by themselves. Serve with the frozen coconut oil candy.

Dietitian's Corner: Xanthan gum is a food thickener. Although it is made from carbohydrate, it does not contribute to the carbohydrate amount in foods because it consists of indigestible fiber. It can also produce a laxative effect, so be careful how much you use at a time and drink plenty of fluids.

PBJ Cookies

CALORIES: 408
4.01:1 RATIO: 2.2 g CARBS

A fun take on peanut butter and jelly! The bread is replaced with a soft, cake-like cookie, and the jelly is replaced with fresh fruit!

_____ 37 g raw egg, mixed well
_____ 20 g macadamia nuts, ground into butter
_____ 11 g canola oil
_____ 5 g flaxseed meal, Bob's Red Mill™
_____ 2 g calorie-free sweetener, Truvia™
_____ 8 g European-style butter
_____ 4 g peanut butter, Skippy Creamy Natural
_____ 4 g strawberries, sliced thin

Preheat the oven to 350°F. After measuring all ingredients on a gram scale, mix the eggs, macadamia nuts, canola oil, flaxseed meal, and Truvia™ together very well. Pour into two or three silicone cupcake liners and bake for about 20 minutes or until cooked thoroughly. While the cookies are baking, mix the peanut butter and butter together until combined. After the cookies are baked and cooled, spread the peanut butter mixture on it like icing. Place the sliced strawberries on top.

Notes: Bake a larger batch of the cookies and freeze each serving in a plastic baggie. On the day you would like to serve them, remove from the freezer and allow to thaw. Top them with the peanut butter and fruit.

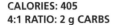

Tuna Salad Boats

CALORIES: 405
4:1 RATIO: 2 g CARBS

This is a fun twist on serving tuna and cucumbers. The mayonnaise is completely eliminated in favor of heart healthy olive oil. As a special treat, Walden Farms chocolate syrup is used to flavor the cream for chocolate milk.

_____ 70 g cucumber, raw, peeled

_____ 30 g canned tuna fish, Bumblebee chunk light in water, drained

_____ 26 g olive oil

_____ 35 g 40% heavy cream

_____ 5 g Walden Farms chocolate syrup

_____ salt/pepper

Hollow out the center of the peeled cucumbers to create a well. Make sure to weigh the cucumbers again to assure that you have the correct weight after removing the seeds. Measure all of the other ingredients. Blend the tuna and the oil together very well. The tuna will hold all of the oil if it is very well drained and mixed. Fill the hollowed out cucumbers with the tuna mixture and season with the salt and pepper. Mix the chocolate syrup and the cream together, add water to make a milk drink.

Notes: A melon-baller works very well to remove the cucumber seeds. Use baby cucumbers if you can find them. It helps to make the meal appear larger in volume!

Fish Sticks with Tartar Sauce

CALORIES: 402
4.02:1 RATIO: 1.8 g CARBS

The breading is omitted from the fish sticks, but this also allows room to serve apple sauce as a flavoring for the oil. Although there is more oil than apple sauce, the oil is flavored enough by the apple sauce that most kids do not mind eating it this way.

_____ 44 g Mahi Mahi, raw
_____ 20 g mayonnaise, Hellman's™
_____ 5 g dill relish, bubbies
_____ 20 g canola oil
_____ 18 g applesauce, Mott's Natural, no sugar added

Measure all ingredients on a gram scale. Slice the fish into "stick" shapes. Spray a nonstick frying pan with spray oil. Lightly fry the fish over medium-low heat until it is cooked thoroughly. Remove the fish to a serving plate. Mix the mayonnaise and relish together and serve with the fish as a dipping sauce. Blend the applesauce and the oil together very well. This may take a minute, but it will hold together once it has been very well blended. Serve immediately.

Salmon Salad

CALORIES: 402
4.01:1 RATIO: 1.9 g CARBS

Salmon salad is a fresh-tasting combination that can be enjoyed at room temperature. If your ratio allows, add some cheese "chips" to scoop up the salad.

_____ 28 g atlantic wild salmon, cooked
_____ 10 g green bell peppers, raw, chopped small
_____ 8 g tomato, raw, chopped small
_____ 7 g yellow bell peppers, raw, chopped small
_____ 3 g scallions, green tops only, chopped small
_____ 37 g 40% heavy cream
_____ 23 g olive oil

Optional: salt/pepper

Measure all ingredients on a gram scale. Break the cooked salmon into small pieces. Add the green and yellow peppers, the scallions, tomatoes, and about half of the olive oil to the salmon. Season with the salt and pepper. Blend the remaining olive oil with the cream and serve as a "milk"-type drink.

Notes: Serve with cheese crackers if your ratio allows. Crackers can be made by sprinkling the cheese into circle shapes, about 1–2 inches in diameter onto a piece of parchment paper. Microwave the cheese on high for about 1 minute. Watch this carefully as it is cooking, and remove from the microwave when the bubbling stops. When the cheese is cool, it should be as crisp as a cracker; if it is still pliable, microwave a few seconds longer. Scrape the remaining fat from the paper onto the chip.

If your ratio allows, vinegar can also be added to create a vinaigrette when mixed with the olive oil.

Fondue with Veggies

CALORIES: 404
4:1 RATIO: 2 g CARBS

The addition of a thick cheese sauce is a great way to get kids to eat their veggies! Low-glycemic vegetables are calculated for this recipe; for lower ratios, you could add carrots or sweet peppers.

_____ 41 g 40% heavy cream
_____ 28.4 g cheese, Kraft Cheddar, block style, grated
_____ 17 g European-style butter
_____ 16 g celery, raw
_____ 14 g cucumber, peeled
_____ 8 g radish, raw

Optional: salt/pepper

Weigh the heavy cream, cheese, and butter in a microwavable bowl. Melt in the microwave in 30-second intervals, about one and half minutes total. Serve with the chopped vegetables on the side to dip in the cheese sauce.

Chicken Salad Sandwich Wrap

CALORIES: 404
4:1 RATIO: 2.1 g CARBS

Just because you cannot have carbs does not mean that you cannot have a sandwich! Egg whites that are beaten stiff then carefully cooked in a nonstick pan make a great substitution for a wrap. This also has the added benefit of adding to the protein of the meal without using any carbohydrate allowance.

_____ 17 g egg whites, whipped into stiff peaks
_____ 15 g chicken breast, cooked, chopped or shredded
_____ 15.5 g mayonnaise, Hellmann's™
_____ 5 g olive oil
_____ 12 g celery, raw, chopped small
_____ salt/pepper
_____ 10 g butterhead lettuce
_____ 11 g green olives, bottled
_____ 50 g 40% heavy cream
_____ 50 g almond milk, Blue Diamond, unsweetened vanilla

Measure all ingredients on a gram scale. Lightly spray a nonstick frying pan with spray oil. With the heat OFF, place the beaten egg whites into the pan and shape it into a flat circle approximately 6–7 inches in diameter and about 1/4–1/2 of an inch thick. Turn the burner on medium-low heat. Cook for about 1 minute until you are able to lift the egg white without it breaking. Flip to cook the other side for about 1 more minute. Set aside on a serving plate to cool.

Combine the chicken breast, celery, mayonnaise, olive oil, and salt and pepper. Mix well to combine. The more finely you chop or shred the chicken, the better it will hold onto the fat. Place the lettuce leaf on the egg white wrap, and add the chicken salad, making sure to scrape the bowl well and roll into a wrap. Serve with the olives on the side. Mix the cream and the almond milk together and serve as a beverage.

Notes: This recipe can easily be converted into a tuna salad wrap by replacing the chicken with canned tuna (must be calculated).

White Chicken Chili
(*Adapted from a recipe submitted by Laurel Moran*)

CALORIES: 406
4:1 RATIO: 2.1 g CARBS

This soup has a great flavor. A small pinch of cumin goes a long way to make a big impact on its flavor. For a spicy version, recalculate to use a jalapeno pepper.

_____ 50 g chicken broth, Imagine free range

_____ 35 g 40% heavy cream

_____ 16 g chicken breast, cooked, diced small

_____ 16 g olive oil

_____ 9 g macadamia nuts

_____ 9 g hass avocado, diced small

_____ 7 g green bell peppers, chopped small

_____ 5 g cheese, Kraft Cheddar, block style, grated

_____ 2 g scallions tops and bottom, sliced thin

_____ 1/4 teaspoon Xanthan gum, add more for a thicker consistency

_____ salt/pepper, pinch of ground cumin

Combine the broth, cream, chicken breast, olive oil, macadamia nuts, peppers, xanthan gum, salt and pepper, and cumin together in a microwavable bowl. Stir very well to combine. Make sure that the xanthan gum is fully incorporated and not lumpy. Microwave for about 1 minute until warmed through. Top the soup with the shredded cheese, diced avocado, and scallions.

Rainbow Trout Roll-Ups

CALORIES: 410
4:1 RATIO: 2.2 g CARBS

This recipe is not nearly as complicated as it looks! Roll-ups are a very fun way to serve simple ingredients.

_____ 29.6 g rainbow trout, cooked, shredded
_____ 20.7 g mayonnaise, Hellmann's™
_____ 12 g cucumber, peeled, sliced into ribbons
_____ 8 g carrots, sliced into ribbons, cooked
_____ 56 g 40% heavy cream

Optional: salt/pepper

Measure all ingredients on a gram scale. Mix the trout, mayonnaise, and optional seasonings together very well. Place a small spoon-full of the mixture onto a serving plate. Wrap the cucumber and carrot around
the mixture to create the roll-ups. Repeat this process until all of the trout mixture and vegetables have been used.

Notes: A vegetable peeler is the best tool to create the "ribbons." Simply run the peeler lengthwise down the vegetables in the same location repeatedly. This will enable you to achieve wide ribbons. Stop when you reach the seeds of the cucumber. For the carrots, after cutting into the ribbon shapes, quickly steam a batch in the microwave, and then weigh out the desired serving.

Cut the lengths of the vegetable ribbons in half lengthwise if smaller size roll-ups are needed.

Simple Chopped Lunch

CALORIES: 400
4:1 RATIO: 1.9 g CARBS

Sometimes all kids want is familiar, simple foods cut into bite-sized pieces. There is no dip, or any fancy combination of ingredients, just bite-sized food served with a "milk" drink.

_____ 25 g egg white, hard boiled
_____ 22 g green olives, canned or bottled
_____ 16 g cheddar cheese, Organic Valley, Raw Sharp Cheddar
_____ 15 g dill pickle, Bubbies
_____ 50 g 40% heavy cream
_____ 11 g walnut oil

Chop all of the ingredients into desired size bite-sized pieces. Arrange on a plate and serve with the cream and oil blended together with water added to make a "milk" drink.

Notes: Ask your dietitian to calculate a different combination of vegetables for your child's food preferences.

Tacos

CALORIES: 401
4:1 RATIO: 1.7 g CARBS

These are a fun keto version of regular tacos that closely resemble the real thing! The cheese is transformed into a crunchy taco shell that kids love.

_____ 14 g cheese, Kraft Cheddar, block style, grated
_____ 14 g 85% lean ground beef, cooked
_____ 10 g mayonnaise, Hellmann's™
_____ 1 g chili powder
_____ 5 g sour cream, full fat
_____ 13 g iceberg lettuce, shredded
_____ 12 g canola oil
_____ 30 g 40% heavy cream, whipped
_____ 3–5 drops of vanilla flavor, Bickford™

Optional: calorie-free sweetener, salt/pepper, Truvia™

After measuring all ingredients on a gram scale, sprinkle the cheese in two circle shapes, about 4 inches in diameter onto a piece of parchment paper. Microwave the cheese on high for about 1 minute. Watch this carefully as it is cooking, remove from the microwave when the bubbling stops. Carefully lift the cheese from the parchment and fold into a taco shell shape. When the cheese is cool, it should be as crisp as a cracker; if it is still pliable, microwave a few seconds longer. Scrape the remaining fat from the paper onto the shell.

Combine the ground beef, mayonnaise, and chili powder together. Mix very well. Place the meat mixture into the taco shell and place the lettuce on the top. Finish with the sour cream.

Tacos (*Continued*)

Mix the whipped cream, canola oil, flavoring and optional Truvia™ together and serve as a vanilla-flavored "pudding."

Notes: The shell can be any size or shape desired. Make several mini tacos for younger children, or shape the cheese into a bowl shape and serve as a taco salad.

Use any kind of hard block cheese. The "harder" the cheese such as Parmesan, less fat will cook out.

Bake and Freeze Pizza

CALORIES: 403
4.01:1 RATIO: 2.1 g CARBS

This pizza is a great all-in-one freezer meal for busy families. The toppings are baked right into the pizza, so it holds together very well for freezing and transporting to school or daycare. Kids love pizza, and this is a nongreasy version that will satisfy any keto kid's pizza cravings!

_____ 30 g egg whites, whipped into stiff peaks
_____ 17 g macadamia nuts, ground into butter
_____ 15 g mayonnaise, Hellmann's™
_____ 13 g olive oil
_____ 14 g canned tomato puree
_____ 9 g Parmesan cheese, block style, grated

Optional: salt/pepper, pinch of garlic powder, pinch of dried Italian herb blend

Preheat the oven to 375°F. After measuring all ingredients on a gram scale, fold the macadamia nuts, mayonnaise, and olive oil into the egg whites. Pour the egg white mixture on a baking sheet lined with a silicone baking mat or piece of parchment paper. Spread into a circle shape about 1/2 an inch thick. Carefully spoon the tomato sauce on the pizza, distributing it as evenly as possible. Sprinkle the grated cheese on top along with the optional seasonings, if desired. Bake for about 20 minutes until the pizza is lightly browned and cooked through. Let the pizza cool on the baking sheet and then serve or freeze.

Notes: If you plan on freezing the pizza, take into account the size of the bag or container you plan on freezing it in. Make two smaller pizzas if necessary. You could also shape it into a standard "slice" shape, like an individual slice of real pizza. Reheat the pizza in the microwave in 30-second intervals.

Meatball Cup

CALORIES: 406
4.01:1 RATIO: 1.8 g CARBS

All the flavor of meatballs and sauce packed into a muffin-sized meal!

_____ 15 g raw egg, mixed well
_____ 12 g mayonnaise, Hellmann's™
_____ 15 g macadamia nuts, ground into a butter
_____ 15 g olive oil
_____ 14 g 85% lean ground beef, cooked
_____ 15 g canned tomato puree
_____ 5 g mozzarella cheese, part skim, grated

After measuring all ingredients on a gram scale, preheat the oven to 350°F. Combine the egg, mayonnaise, macadamia nuts, olive oil, and salt/pepper. Mix well and pour into two silicone muffin liners. Spread half of the sauce on the top of each muffin, and then sprinkle the cheese and Italian seasonings on top. Bake for about 20 minutes until cooked thoroughly.

Keto "Hamburger Helper"

CALORIES: 399
4:1 RATIO: 1.5 g CARBS

Creamy and cheesy, the spaghetti squash is very well disguised by the cheese, so picky eaters may never even notice they are eating it!

_____ 20 g 85% lean ground beef, cooked
_____ 20 g 40% heavy cream
_____ 21.2 g mayonnaise, Hellmann's™
_____ 10 g European-style butter
_____ 10 g Kraft Cheddar cheese, block style, grated
_____ 11 g spaghetti squash, cooked
_____ salt/pepper

After measuring all ingredients on a gram scale, combine in a small nonstick skillet. Heat on medium heat until the cheese is melted and all the ingredients have combined. Do not overcook or bring to a boil, this will cause the sauce to "break" and the oil to separate.

Notes: To better disguise the squash, cook it until it is very soft and then chop it very fine.

Pot Roast

CALORIES: 406
4:1 RATIO: 1.8 g CARBS

This is a great example of how a keto meal can be prepared along with the family meal. Place the beef chuck, carrots, onion, potato, and mushrooms in a roasting pan. Add a small amount of water to cover the bottom. Salt and pepper to taste. Cover and cook in a 325°F oven for 4 hours. Remove the cover and cook for one more hour. Remove and weigh the keto portion of the beef and carrots, and then season the remaining meal to the families' desired taste.

_____ 43 g 40% heavy cream
_____ 23 g beef chuck roast, cooked
_____ 12 g carrots, cooked
_____ 10.7 g European-style butter
_____ 11 g walnut oil

After measuring all ingredients on a gram scale, place the beef and carrots in a small dish and add the butter. Serve the cream with added water to make a "milk" drink. Pour the oil in a small cup to drink.

Dietitian's Corner: Walnut oil is high in polyunsaturated fatty acids, which can lower blood cholesterol levels.

Beef and Spaghetti Squash in Alfredo Sauce

CALORIES: 404
4.02:1 RATIO: 2 g CARBS

This meal comes together in a flash with ingredients that have been cooked in advance. All that is needed is to heat it in the microwave and you have a warm, cheesy meal with kid-pleasing flavors.

_____ 30 g 40% heavy cream
_____ 15 g spaghetti squash, cooked
_____ 19 g 85% lean ground beef, cooked
_____ 13.5 g mayonnaise, Hellmann's™
_____ 6 g Parmesan cheese, block style, grated
_____ 13 g olive oil

Optional: salt/pepper, pinch of dried parsley flakes

After measuring all ingredients on a gram scale, combine the heavy cream, squash, beef, mayonnaise, cheese, and 3 grams of the olive oil together in a microwavable bowl. Heat on high for about 30 seconds, and then stir and heat in 30-second intervals until the sauce has thickened. Serve the 10 additional grams of oil in a medicine syringe.

Beef Mole

CALORIES: 404
4:1 RATIO: 2.1 g CARBS

Mole is a traditional Mexican dish that combines chili peppers, tomatoes, and chocolate to create a full flavored, dark brown sauce. This flavor combination is easy to make and a welcome new flavor to discover. Grilled flank steak would be an excellent substitution for the ground beef.

_____ 30 g 40% heavy cream, whipped
_____ 15 g walnut oil
_____ 16 g canned tomato puree
_____ 1 g chili powder
_____ 25 g 85% lean ground beef, cooked
_____ 2 g baker's unsweetened chocolate squares, chopped fine
_____ 9.6 g European-style butter

Optional: salt/pepper, 3–5 drops of vanilla flavor, Bickford™, liquid sweetener

After measuring all ingredients on a gram scale, combine the whipped cream and walnut oil in a small bowl and mix well. Add the optional vanilla flavor and sweetener if desired. Set aside and serve as a vanilla flavored "pudding."

Combine the tomato puree, chili powder, beef, chocolate, and butter in a small microwavable bowl. Heat in 30-second intervals on high until the sauce is hot. Mix well and serve.

Carbonara

CALORIES: 401
4.01:1 RATIO: 2 g CARBS

*Keto carbonara is made using a product called Tofu shirataki noodles.
These are a pasta substitute that some people enjoy on low-carb diets.
They tend to have a "rubbery" type texture, so please cut them up into
shorter lengths before serving to kids!*

_____ 22 g 40% heavy cream

_____ 24 g raw egg, mixed well

_____ 15 g European-style butter

_____ 14 g mayonnaise, Hellmann's™

_____ 34 g tofu shirataki noodles

_____   6 g Parmesan cheese, block style, grated

_____   6 g bacon, Smithfield, no sugar added, cooked

Optional: salt/pepper, pinch of garlic powder, pinch of dried parsley

After measuring all ingredients on a gram scale, combine the
heavy cream, raw egg, and butter in a microwavable bowl.
Heat in 15-second increments on high, stirring well each time,
until the mixture reaches 160°F. If the eggs begin to scramble,
use an immersion blender to smooth out the sauce. Stir in the
mayonnaise, optional seasonings, and noodles. Sprinkle the top
with the cheese and bacon.

Notes: For lower ratios, add more noodles or some sautéed
mushrooms.

This recipe makes a generous amount of sauce.

Use spaghetti squash in place of the Shiritaki if desired.

Chicken Curry Pattie

CALORIES: 403
4:1 RATIO: 2 g CARBS

A flavor twist on the chicken nugget! The curry powder is not spicy; it is a great mild, warming spice that may become a new favorite! Make sure that you buy a curry powder that has no added ingredients or fillers.

_____ 25 g macadamia nuts, ground into butter
_____ 17 g canola oil
_____ 15 g chicken breast, cooked, shredded
_____ 10 g egg whites, raw, whipped into stiff peaks
_____ 1 g curry powder
_____ 20 g coconut milk, Thai Kitchen unsweetened, full fat

Optional: salt/pepper

Measure all ingredients on a gram scale. Fold the macadamia nuts, walnut oil, chicken, curry powder, and optional seasonings into the egg whites. Spray a nonstick frying pan with spray oil. Make about 3 mounds of the chicken batter and fry on each side for about 1 minute over medium-low heat. When the edges look slightly dry, flip to cook the other side. Continue cooking until cooked all the way through. Remove patties to a serving plate and scrape the remaining fat out of the pan onto the patties. Serve the coconut milk on the side as a dipping sauce or as a beverage.

Dietitian's Corner: Coconut milk is a dairy-free milk alternative, making this recipe safe for children with milk allergies.

BBQ Pork Shoulder and Coleslaw

CALORIES: 405
4:1 RATIO: 2 g CARBS

All the flavor of BBQ without any of the sugary BBQ sauce! Coleslaw is served as a crunchy and refreshing side.

For the coleslaw:

———— 29 g green cabbage, raw and shredded
———— 17 g mayonnaise, Hellmann's™
———— 11 g 40% heavy cream
———— 1 g cider vinegar
———— 1 g calorie-free sweetener, Truvia™
———— salt/pepper

After measuring all ingredients on a gram scale, mix together very well. Set aside in a covered bowl to allow the cabbage to soften slightly.

For the BBQ pork:

———— 31 g pork shoulder, cooked
———— 16 g European-style butter
———— 2 g chili powder
———— 1 g cider vinegar
———— 1 g Truvia™
———— 7 g avocado, Hass
———— salt/pepper

Measure all ingredients on a gram scale. Shred the pork very finely and add the butter. Melt the butter in the microwave. Add the chili powder, vinegar, Truvia™, and salt/pepper. Mix very well to combine all the ingredients. Serve the pork with the avocado and coleslaw as sides.

BBQ Pork Shoulder and Coleslaw (*Continued*)

Notes: If you do not like avocado, mash it into a smooth puree with a fork and mix it into the coleslaw. The vinegar in the coleslaw will prevent it from browning. You will never be able to guess it is in there!

Cook an entire plain pork shoulder in the crock pot. Remove the amount needed for the keto meal and season the rest of the meat for the family.

Crab Cakes and Tartar Sauce

CALORIES: 402
4:1 RATIO: 0.8 g CARBS

Crab cakes are keto friendly and also make quite a large portion!

_____ 31 g crab meat, white lump from blue crab, canned
_____ 26 g egg whites, whipped into stiff peaks
_____ 15 g canola oil
_____ 10 g European-style butter
_____ 20 g mayonnaise, Hellmann's™
_____ 10 g relish, bubbies
_____ 32 g celery, raw

After measuring all ingredients on a gram scale, fold the crab meat and canola oil into the egg whites. Melt the butter in a nonstick frying pan. Make 3–4 crab cakes in the pan and fry them similar to a pancake. When the edges are slightly browned and cooked, flip them over to cook the other side. Cook them until they are cooked thoroughly and move them to a serving plate. Scrape all of the fat out of the pan onto the crab cakes. Mix the mayonnaise and the relish together and serve as a dipping sauce. Serve the celery on the side.

Notes: If an all-in-one style meal is desired, simply chop the celery very fine and mix all of the ingredients together. Cook by the same method and serve.

Add a pinch of seafood seasoning, such as Old Bay, to add a bit of extra flavor to the crab cakes.

If your ratio allows, swap out the tartar sauce for "cocktail" sauce by mixing horseradish with low-sugar ketchup.

Teriyaki Salmon Cakes

CALORIES: 400
4:1 RATIO: 1.5 g CARBS

There is no need to cook the Swiss chard before eating. Lightly dress it with a splash of vinegar, salt, and pepper. The heat of the salmon cakes will slightly wilt the greens and make them more tender.

_____ 20 g Swiss chard, raw, shredded fine
_____ 21.2 g Wild Atlantic salmon, cooked
_____ 15 g macadamia nuts, ground into butter
_____ 15 g mayonnaise, Hellmann's™
_____ 10 g raw egg, mixed well
_____ 4 g soy sauce, Kikkoman naturally brewed
_____ 3 g sesame oil, refined
_____ 0.1 g kelp granules, sea seasonings
_____ 13 g European-style butter
_____ salt/pepper

Measure all ingredients on a gram scale. Place the shredded Swiss chard on a serving plate. Mix the salmon, macadamia nuts, mayonnaise, egg, soy sauce, sesame oil, and sea kelp together very well. Melt the butter in a nonstick frying pan over medium heat. Drop 3–4 patties of the salmon mixture into the pan and fry until the sides begin to turn slightly brown. Flip to cook the other side, about 1 minute. Cook until the cakes are cooked thoroughly, about 3 minutes total. Remove the cooked salmon cakes from the pan and place on top of the Swiss chard. Scrape all of the remaining fat out of the pan onto the cakes.

Dietitian's Corner: Many people with nut allergies will also have an allergy to sesame seeds. In this recipe, you can replace the sesame oil with any other oil such as canola oil.

Pork Stir Fry with Ginger Cream Soda

CALORIES: 406
4.01:1 RATIO: 2 g CARBS

If your family lies to go out to eat, this would be a fun keto meal to bring along. Restaurants are often able to serve plain carbonated water. Ask for a glass to add the cream and create a fun cream soda!

_____ 22.5 g pork tenderloin, sliced very thin, then cooked
_____ 13 g broccoli, cooked
_____ 2 g soy sauce, Kikkoman naturally brewed
_____ 3 g sesame oil, refined
_____ 0.5 g sesame seeds, dried
_____ 16 g walnut oil
_____ 50 g 40% heavy cream
_____ 1 g calorie-free sweetener, Truvia™
_____ 0.5 g ground ginger, powder variety from the spice isle

After measuring all ingredients, combine the pork, broccoli, soy sauce, sesame oil, and 6 g of the walnut oil. Mix well to combine. Sprinkle the sesame seeds on top. Blend the dried ginger, Truvia™, and the remaining walnut oil into the cream, and top with ice and carbonated water to make a "cream soda."

Notes: If you would like to serve this in a travel container, make sure that you are able to scrape out the fat and that it will not be absorbed (i.e., do not use a cardboard or paper-lined container that may absorb that fat).

Sautéed Lamb with Pomegranate, Feta, and Walnuts

CALORIES: 401
4:1 RATIO: 1.9 g CARBS

A fancy keto dinner that can be quickly prepared! If you have never tried lamb meat before, dont be nervous! Lamb offers a welcome change of flavor to the same old chicken, beef, or pork.

_____ 19.8 g mayonnaise, Hellmann's™	_____ 13 g 40% heavy cream
_____ 1 g fresh squeezed lemon juice	_____ 0.5 g fresh parsley
	_____ salt/pepper
_____ 20 g lamb tenderloin, pounded very thin, cooked	_____ 10 g European-style butter
_____ 10 g European-style butter	_____ 7.5 g feta cheese
_____ 7 g black walnuts, dried	_____ 5 g pomegranate seeds, fresh

After measuring all ingredients on a gram scale, mix together the mayonnaise, heavy cream, lemon juice, parsley, salt, and pepper. Pour the mixture onto a serving plate and set aside. Melt the butter in a nonstick frying pan and reheat the lamb meat in the butter. The lamb will absorb some of the butter by using this method. Remove the lamb and place on top of the mayonnaise sauce. Scrape all of the remaining butter out of the pan onto the lamb. Crumble the feta and walnuts and sprinkle over the top of the meat. Finish by sprinkling the pomegranate seeds over the top.

Notes: If you have never removed the seeds from a fresh pomegranate before, here are some tips to help. First, remove the top of the pomegranate and score into sections on the thickest areas of the membrane with a knife. Then place the fruit in a bowl of water and pull open the sections and release the seeds. After removing the membranes from the water, drain and dry the excess water from the seeds using a paper towel.

Shrimp Curry

CALORIES: 405
4.01:1 RATIO: 1.9 g CARBS

Shrimp curry is creamy and delicious. Although the flavor of curry is strong, it is not spicy or overpowering. In fact, this comes to our advantage when serving Brussels sprouts, which many kids do not enjoy; when combined with a curry, they just might decide they like them!

- _____ 40 g coconut milk, Thai Kitchen, full fat, unsweetened
- _____ 15 g mayonnaise, Hellmann's™
- _____ 15 g European-style butter
- _____ 8 g coconut oil
- _____ 1 g curry powder
- _____ 34.5 g shrimp, steamed
- _____ 13 g brussels sprouts, cooked
- _____ salt/pepper

Measure all ingredients on a gram scale. In a microwave-safe bowl, mix together the coconut milk, mayonnaise, butter, coconut oil, curry powder, and salt and pepper and heat in a microwave until warm, about 1 minute. Stir the sauce again to create a smooth consistency. Dice the shrimp and Brussels sprouts into bite-sized pieces and mix into the curry sauce.

Notes: If your child has a shellfish allergy, or is not fond of shrimp, ask your dietitian to create a recipe that substitutes it with chicken, beef, pork, or tofu.

Cabbage Bolognese

CALORIES: 405
4:1 RATIO: 2.1 g CARBS

A take on traditional Pasta Bolognese with cabbage as the noodles! If your ratio allows, calculate in some Parmesan cheese.

_____ 21 g green cabbage, cooked, shredded

_____ 25.5 g 85% lean ground beef, cooked

_____ 31 g 40% heavy cream

_____ 15 g European-style butter

_____ 10 g canned tomato puree

_____ 6.5 g olive oil

_____ 6 g mayonnaise, Hellmann's™

_____ salt/pepper, pinch of Italian seasonings

Measure all ingredients and mix together in a microwave-safe bowl. Heat for about 1 minute or until desired temperature is reached. Stir very well to combine the ingredients and serve.

Chicken Tetrazzini

CALORIES: 403
4:1 RATIO 1.8 g CARBS

This tetrazzini is made with Tofu shirataki noodles. Shirataki is a low-carbohydrate pasta replacement that some people enjoy on low-carb diets. They have a "rubbery"-type texture, so be sure to cut them into shorter lengths when serving to children.

_____ 15 g European-style butter

_____ 10 g olive oil

_____ 8 g white mushrooms, raw, sliced thin

_____ 16 g chicken breast, cooked, diced

_____ 39 g 40% heavy cream

_____ 16 g tofu shirataki noodles, prepared according to package direction, cut into short lengths

_____ 6 g Parmesan cheese, block style, grated

_____ salt/pepper, pinch of garlic powder

Measure all ingredients on a gram scale. In a small nonstick frying pan, melt the butter and the olive oil over medium-low heat. Sauté the sliced mushrooms until tender. Add the cooked chicken breast and sauté another minute. Turn the heat down to low and add the remaining ingredients. Carefully heat until warmed through and the sauce has combined and thickened. Pour the mixture onto a serving plate and scrape all of the remaining sauce out of the pan onto the plate.

Notes: If you would like to omit the shiritaki, fill the carb allotment with more mushrooms or spaghetti squash.

Chicken Enchilada Casserole

CALORIES: 406
4.01:1 RATIO: 1.8 G CARBS

If you are not familiar with tomatillos, they look like a green tomato covered in a papery husk. They are most often cooked prior to eating and are typical of southwestern style foods. They have a great, tart flavor and are the basis for a green (verde) salsa.

_____ 15 g European-style butter
_____ 14 g tomatillo, diced small
_____ 20 g chicken breast, cooked, diced
_____ 16 g mayonnaise, Hellmann's™
_____ 31 g 40% heavy cream
_____ 5 g cheese, Kraft Cheddar, block style, grated
_____ 3 g scallions, sliced thin
_____ 1 g fresh Cilantro
_____ salt/pepper

Measure all ingredients on a gram scale. In a small nonstick frying pan, melt the butter over medium-low heat. Add the chopped tomatillos and sauté for about 1 minute until they begin to soften. Add the chicken breast and cook for 1 more minute. Add the remaining ingredients and reduce the heat to low. Stir to combine and heat until the cheese has melted. Pour the mixture onto a serving plate and scrape all of the remaining sauce out of the pan onto the serving plate.

Broccoli, Bacon, and Blue Cheese Melt

CALORIES: 406
4:1 RATIO: 2 g CARBS

A delicious savory combination with strong flavors! If you are cooking for a crowd, the broccoli and melted blue cheese makes a great side dish for the rest of the family.

_____ 50 g 40% heavy cream
_____ 24 g broccoli, cooked
_____ 12 g bacon, Smithfield, no sugar added, cooked, crumbled
_____ 11 g olive oil
_____ 10 g blue cheese, crumbled

Optional: salt/pepper

After measuring all ingredients on a gram scale, combine half of the heavy cream with the broccoli, crumbled bacon, olive oil, and blue cheese in a microwavable bowl. Heat in the microwave until the cheese has melted and is warmed through, in 30-second intervals. Stir to combine the cream, oil, and cheese to create the sauce. Add the salt and pepper if desired.

Notes: You can easily replace the bacon with grilled beef tenderloin in this recipe, and you will need to recalculate the recipe to increase the meat and fat if you use a lean cut.

Serve some of the oil on the side if preferred.

103

Sushi

CALORIES: 409
4:1 RATIO: 2.2 g CARBS

It would seem as though eating sushi would not even be a possibility while on the ketogenic diet. However, the only real culprit in traditional sushi is the rice. Rice is often replaced with cauliflower on low carb diets, and there is no reason why the same logic would not apply to this meal!

_____ 45 g cauliflower, steamed, shredded or "riced"
_____ 20 g raw egg whites, beaten stiff
_____ 26.4 g canola oil
_____ 1.5 g nori, Eden Brand
_____ 11 g yellow fin tuna, cooked
_____ 12 g avocado, Hass, sliced thin
_____ 3 g soy sauce, Kikkoman low sodium
_____ 30.5 g 40% heavy cream, whipped
_____ pinch of powdered ginger

Optional: Liquid sweetener, vanilla flavor, Bickford™

Preheat the oven to 350°F. Measure all ingredients on a gram scale. Fold the cauliflower and 10 g canola oil into the egg whites. Mix very well to combine. Scoop the egg and cauliflower mixture onto a silicone-lined baking sheet. Form it into a "log" shape approximately the same length as the nori. Bake in the oven for 15–20 minutes or until the mixture is cooked thoroughly. Allow the "rice" to cool, carefully lift the "rice" off of the baking sheet and place it on the nori. Add the cooked tuna and sliced avocado to the center of the roll and then carefully roll up the nori to create the sushi roll. Set the roll on a cutting board seam side down to help the nori form a seal. Place the roll in the freezer for an hour; then with a very sharp knife, slice the roll into bite-sized pieces. Arrange the sliced sushi on a serving plate and drizzle the weighed soy sauce on top.

Sushi (*Continued*)

Mix the whipped cream with the powdered ginger, the remaining 16.4 g canola oil, and optional ingredients and freeze for a minimum of 15 minutes. Serve as "ice cream" for a dessert. If the ice cream is made in advance, remove it from the freezer 15–20 minutes before eating.

Notes: Ask your dietitian to calculate in different sushi fillings such as salmon, eggs, shrimp, lettuce, or cucumbers. A "spicy" roll could be created using mayonnaise and hot sauce.

Feel free to replace some of the canola oil with toasted sesame oil to dip the sushi; this oil has a string, nutty flavor.

Pop "Unders"

CALORIES: 150
4:1 RATIO: 1.4 g CARBS

Makes 1 pop-under

This snack is inspired by traditional popovers and is prepared in a similar fashion. The keto version has too much fat to "pop over" and instead creates a hollow center that is perfect for filling with whipped cream!

———— 7.5 g European-style butter
———— 13 g raw egg, mixed well
———— 9 g coconut milk, full fat
———— 2 g coconut flour, Bob's Red Mill™
———— 13 g 40% heavy cream, whipped
———— 1 g calorie-free sweetener, Truvia™

Optional: salt, 3–5 drops of vanilla flavor, Bickford™

After measuring all ingredients, preheat the oven to 350°F. Place the butter in a muffin tin lined with a silicone baking cup and place it into the oven to melt the butter. In a separate bowl, combine the egg, coconut milk, coconut flour, salt, and optional flavorings together and mix well. Remove the preheated muffin tin from the oven and pour the batter into the melted butter. Do not stir! Return to the oven and cook for about 15 minutes. Let the pop-under cool in the silicone liner to reabsorb the butter. Fold the sweetener into the whipped cream and fill the hollow center.

Notes: Replace the whipped cream topping with a combination of coconut oil, butter, and cocoa powder to make a chocolate sauce.

Cinnamon Sugar Pecans

CALORIES: 151
4:1 RATIO: 1.5 g CARBS

This is a rare, exciting treat where real sugar can be used. The tiny amount goes a long way and makes plain pecans a special snack. This also great to eat on the go because it is not messy at all!

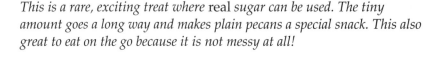

_____ 21 g pecans
_____ 3.2 g raw egg white
_____ 0.5 g white sugar, granulated
_____ 0.3 g cinnamon, ground

After measuring all ingredients, combine all the ingredients in a small mixing bowl and stir to evenly coat the pecans. Using a small spatula, place the pecans on a baking sheet lined with a silicone mat or parchment paper. Scrape all the remaining egg whites out of the bowl onto the pecans. Try not to let the pecans touch each other! Bake in a 325°F oven for about 15 minutes. Allow to cool, then store in a small air-tight container.

CALORIES: 153
4:1 RATIO: 1.8 g CARBS

A combination of three ordinary ingredients transforms into special keto cookies perfect for any holiday or celebration. Baking intensifies the natural sweetness of the fruit, so no additional sweetener is needed.

_____ 20 g roasted macadamia nuts, ground
_____ 14.4 g raspberries, pureed
_____   3 g raw egg whites

Optional: pinch of salt, 3–5 drops of vanilla flavor, Bickford™

After measuring all ingredients, combine the macadamia nuts, egg whites, and optional ingredients and mix well. Divide the mixture into three sections of an oven-safe silicone candy mold (see Equipment and Utensils on page 7). Press the nut mixture evenly into the molds and then form an indentation in the cookie to hold the fruit puree. Lightly oiled fingers will help prevent the nut mixture from sticking. Spoon the fruit puree into the indentations and bake in a 350°F oven for 15 minutes or until lightly browned and crisp.

Notes: Use any fruit puree that is preferred. Frozen fruit works very well for baked recipes.

Chocolate Cupcakes

CALORIES: 151
4:1 RATIO: 1.2 g CARBS

Makes 1 cupcake

Easy to make cupcakes with a light, spongy texture.

_____ 13 g egg whites, whipped into stiff peaks
_____ 7.7 g European-style butter
_____ 7 g coconut oil
_____ 4 g flaxseed meal, Bob's Red Mill™
_____ 2.3 g hershey's unsweetened cocoa powder
_____ 2 g calorie-free sweetener, Truvia™
_____ 0.1 g calumet baking powder

Optional: 3–5 drops of flavors such as vanilla or chocolate, Bickford™, pinch of salt

After measuring all ingredients, melt the butter and coconut oil in a small mixing bowl. Stir in the flaxseed meal, cocoa powder, Truvia™, baking powder, and optional flavors and salt. Fold in the egg whites and mix carefully until combined. Pour batter into a silicone cupcake liner and bake in a 350°F oven for 15 minutes.

Notes: This is a great recipe to make in a large batch. Multiply each ingredient by the number of desired servings and make the batter. Fill each cupcake liner with the total number of grams of each ingredient for every serving.

Omit the cocoa powder and calculate in sugar-free jelly for a jelly-filled-type cupcake.

Jell-O® Puffs

CALORIES: 154
4:1 RATIO: 0.7 g CARBS

Jell-O®-flavored puffs are a great snack to bring anywhere on the go. They are a nongreasy, snackable treat that is very easy to eat even for very young children.

———— 15.6 g egg whites, whipped into stiff peaks
———— 13 g pecans, ground very fine
———— 6 g walnut oil
———— 0.5 g sugar-free Jell-O® powder

After measuring all ingredients, fold the pecans, walnut oil, and Jell-O® into the egg whites. Mix just enough to combine the ingredients. Do not over mix, so not to lose the volume of the egg whites.

Scrape the mixture into a small resealable sandwich baggie. Press the air out of the bag and seal. Snip the bottom corner off of one side of the bag creating an opening about 1/4 of an inch. Pipe "dime"-sized mounds of the batter onto a parchment- or silicone-lined baking sheet and bake in a 300°F oven for about 10–12 minutes or until they are dry all the way through. If they begin to brown, turn the oven heat down. Allow to cool on the baking sheet and store in an air-tight container.

Brazil Nut Cookies

CALORIES: 154
4.01:1 RATIO: 1 g CARBS

Brazil nuts are a plentiful natural source of selenium, but not usually a favorite of most kids. This cookie version creates a delicious, crunchy cookie that kids will look forward to eating!

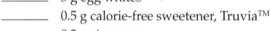

_____ 18 g Brazil nuts, ground fine
_____ 3.7 g coconut oil
_____ 3 g egg whites
_____ 0.5 g calorie-free sweetener, Truvia™
_____ 0.2 g cinnamon

Optional: 3–5 drops of vanilla flavor, Bickford™, pinch of salt

After measuring all ingredients, mix together all the ingredients very well. Divide the nut mixture into 4–5 equal portions. Roll into small ball shapes and flatten with a fork, or press into an oven-safe silicone candy mold shape. Bake in a 350°F oven for 15 minutes.

Dietitian's Corner: Selenium is an essential trace mineral, classified as an antioxidant. Selenium deficiency can occur with the ketogenic diet due to the restrictiveness of the food options.

No-Bake Tropical Cream Cheese Bars

CALORIES: 153
4:1 RATIO: 2.2 g CARBS

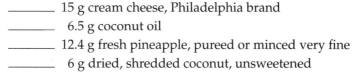

Large amounts of pineapple are not easily used on the ketogenic diet. The flavor and natural sweetness of the pineapple is highlighted in this easy to make treat. Make in batches and freeze.

_____ 15 g cream cheese, Philadelphia brand
_____ 6.5 g coconut oil
_____ 12.4 g fresh pineapple, pureed or minced very fine
_____ 6 g dried, shredded coconut, unsweetened

Optional: 3–5 drops of flavor such as Pina Colada, Bickford™

After measuring all ingredients, melt the cream cheese and coconut oil together in a small mixing bowl. Add the pineapple and coconut and stir very well to combine. Spoon into silicone candy molds or spread on wax paper. Freeze until the mixture has hardened. Store each serving in a plastic baggie in the freezer. These will soften if allowed to come to room temperature.

No-Bake Chocolate Snack Bars

CALORIES: 152
4:1 RATIO: 1.6 g CARBS

Tastes like rich dark chocolate! A quick combination of ingredients creates a special chocolate treat!

_____	5.5 g unsweetened baker's chocolate
_____	5 g coconut oil
_____	3 g calorie-free sweetener, Truvia™
_____	2 g sunflower seeds, dry roasted
_____	4 g Brazil nuts, ground
_____	5 g pecans, ground

After measuring all ingredients, combine in a small microwaveable bowl. Heat until the coconut oil and chocolate have melted, about 30 seconds. Mix very well and spread on a sheet of wax paper. Freeze until hardened and break into bite-sized pieces. Store in plastic baggies in the freezer. This will melt at room temperature.

Notes: A liquid sweetener will incorporate easier than a powdered type.

Apples and Peanut Butter Dip

CALORIES: 152
4:1 RATIO: 2.7 g CARBS

Apples and peanut butter are a familiar, well-liked combination by many kids. Here is how to enjoy them on the ketogenic diet.

_____ 7 g coconut oil
_____ 7 g European-style butter
_____ 5 g peanut butter, Skippy Creamy Natural
_____ 17.7 g apple, no skin, sliced thin

Optional: 3–5 drops of flavors, such as caramel or chocolate, Bickford™

After measuring all ingredients, combine the coconut oil, butter, and peanut butter in a small microwavable bowl. Heat until melted, about 30 seconds. Stir the mixture well to combine. Add optional flavorings if using. It will be the consistency of a thick liquid after heating. Allow it to cool to room temperature and it will thicken into a "peanut butter" consistency. Serve with the sliced apple.

Notes: You could also mince the apples very fine and freeze the mixture in silicone candy molds.

No-Cook Almond Butter Pudding

CALORIES: 150
4.03:1 RATIO: 1.2 g CARBS

This is a quick snack with very smooth, easy-to-eat texture. It is not a large quantity, so it is useful when recovering from illness or for kids with a small appetite.

_____ 9 g almond butter, Maranatha organic creamy roasted
_____ 26 g 40% heavy cream, whipped

After measuring all ingredients, soften the almond butter for a few seconds in the microwave. Add 5 g of the whipped cream and stir very well to "loosen" the almond butter. Fold in the remaining whipped cream and serve.

Notes: You can recalculate the recipe to use different nut butters.

Basic "Sugar" Cookies

CALORIES: 152
4.01:1 RATIO: 1.7 g CARBS

A very mild, soft texture cookie that is easy to make in large batches.

_____ 5.5 g Coconut flour, Bob's Red Mill™
_____ 10 g Raw egg, mixed well
_____ 8 g Coconut oil
_____ 7 g European-style butter
_____ 2 g Calorie-free sweetener, Truvia™

Optional: 3–5 drops of vanilla flavor, Bickford™

After measuring all ingredients, melt the butter and coconut oil. Add the remaining ingredients and stir very well. Divide the batter into three silicone baking cups or six mini silicone baking cups. Bake in a 350°F oven for 10–15 minutes or until lightly browned on the edges.

Notes: Add fresh fruit on the top of the cookies before baking for lower ratio needs.

Cheese Crackers

CALORIES: 151
4:1 RATIO: 1 g CARBS

Cheese crackers are always a hit. Mix up a batch and send them to school!

_____ 18 g macadamia nuts, ground into butter

_____ 4.5 g cheese, Kraft Cheddar, block style, grated

_____ 3 g egg whites

_____ pinch of salt

After measuring all ingredients, mix together and drop "dime" size spoonfuls onto a silicone- or parchment-lined baking sheet. Bake in a 350°F oven for about 7–10 minutes or until lightly browned around the edges.

Notes: Using a "sharp" or strong flavored cheese will provide a better cheese flavor.

Chocolate Custard

CALORIES: 152
4:1 RATIO: 1 g CARBS

This chocolate custard is smooth textured and easy to make in large batches.

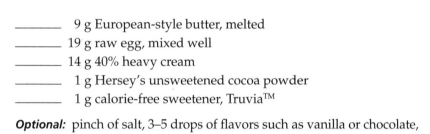

_____	9 g European-style butter, melted
_____	19 g raw egg, mixed well
_____	14 g 40% heavy cream
_____	1 g Hersey's unsweetened cocoa powder
_____	1 g calorie-free sweetener, Truvia™

Optional: pinch of salt, 3–5 drops of flavors such as vanilla or chocolate, Bickford™

Preheat the oven to 350°F. Boil a kettle of water. After measuring all ingredients, combine and pour into a lightly greased custard dish. Place the custard dish in a shallow casserole pan and fill the casserole pan with boiling water about half way up the sides of the custard dish. Carefully place in the oven and bake for about 20 minutes. You can tell when the custard is done by gently shaking the custard. If the center is still liquid, cook 5 minutes longer or until the center is firm.

Cheese-Filled Olives

CALORIES: 154
4:1 RATIO: 0.4 g CARBS

The creaminess of the goat cheese or Chevre *cuts the sharp, briny flavor of the olives nicely. This snack has a very sophisticated taste and appearance!*

_____ 30 g green olives, bottled
_____ 13.4 g goat cheese
_____ 7 g olive oil

Optional: salt/pepper, pinch of cayenne pepper

After measuring all ingredients on a gram scale, slice the olives in half lengthwise. Spread a small amount of the cheese on the top of each half. Drizzle the olive oil over the cheese and olives and then sprinkle with the optional ingredients.

Vanilla Cupcakes

CALORIES: 151
4.01:1 RATIO: 1.4 g CARBS

Makes 1 cupcake

Light and fluffy vanilla cupcakes that taste very similar to the store bought box mixes!

_____ 16 g raw egg whites, beaten stiff
_____ 10.4 g walnut oil
_____ 5 g European-style butter, melted
_____ 4.2 g coconut flour, Bob's Red Mill™
_____ 1.5 g calorie-free sweetener, Truvia™
_____ 0.2 g baking powder
_____ 3–5 drops of vanilla flavor, Bickford™

Preheat oven to 350°F. After measuring all ingredients on a gram scale, carefully fold the oil, melted butter, coconut flour, Truvia™, baking powder, and vanilla flavor into the egg whites. You do not want to deflate the egg whites; this is what gives the cupcake its fluffy texture. Pour the batter into a silicone cupcake liner and bake for about 15 minutes or until cooked thoroughly.

Notes: Replace some of the oil with sweetened, flavored whipped cream, butter or whipped vegetable shortening as a frosting if desired.

Fudge Popsicle

CALORIES: 151
4:1 RATIO: 1.9 g CARBS

Makes 1 popsicle

You better make this after the kids go to bed so you don't give away the secret ingredient! Avocado is the main ingredient cleverly disguised by chocolate and sweetener. Freezing the popsicle also helps to hide the avocado flavor.

_____ 50 g avocado, pureed *very smooth* in a food processor
_____ 4 g coconut oil
_____ 6 g unsweetened bakers chocolate squares
_____ 3.5 g calorie-free sweetener, Truvia™
_____ 3–5 drops of vanilla flavor, Bickford™

After measuring all ingredients on a gram scale, melt the coconut oil and chocolate together in the microwave. Add the avocado, Truvia™, and vanilla flavor. Stir very well to combine. Pour into a popsicle mold, place a wooden popsicle stick in the center of the pop, and freeze overnight. Once frozen, run the underside popsicle mold under hot tap water for a few seconds to loosen the pop. Remove the pops and store in plastic baggies in the freezer.

Notes: This does not have to be frozen to enjoy; this can be served immediately as a smooth chocolate pudding. For those who require a lower ratio, eliminate the oil or add pureed banana for extra favor.

Veggies and Dip

CALORIES: 154
4.01:1 RATIO: 2.6 g CARBS

A simple combination of mayonnaise and cream cheese make a great tasting dip for serving veggies!

———— 14 g mayonnaise, Hellmann's™
———— 12 g cream cheese, Philadelphia brand
———— 14 g jicama, peeled, sliced into sticks
———— 14 g cucumber, peeled, sliced into sticks
———— 10.2 g carrots, peeled, sliced into sticks
———— 5 g radish, sliced into thin rounds

Measure all ingredients on a gram scale. Mix the mayonnaise and cream cheese together very well. Place the sliced veggies on a plate to dip into the mayonnaise/cream cheese mixture. Make sure you scrape all of the dip out of the bowl to finish eating the snack.

Pumpkin Seed Muffins

CALORIES: 152
4.01:1 RATIO: 1.1 g CARBS

Makes 1 muffin

Pumpkin seeds are a surprising ingredient in this muffin! You can find pumpkin seeds, sometimes labeled pepitas, in the international food isle in grocery stores. These are not the same variety as pumpkin seeds from jack-o-lantern pumpkins; they have a green color and a skinny, oblong shape.

_____ 11 g egg whites, whipped into stiff peaks
_____ 6 g pumpkin seeds, dried, ground into "flour"
_____ 5 g mayonnaise, Hellmann's™
_____ 5 g coconut oil, melted
_____ 3 g calorie-free sweetener, Truvia™
_____ 0.1 g baking powder
_____ 4 g European-style butter, room temperature for serving

Preheat the oven to 350°F. Measure all ingredients on a gram scale. Fold the pumpkin seeds, mayonnaise, coconut oil, Truvia™, and baking powder into the egg whites. Mix well to combine and pour the mixture into a silicone baking cup. Bake in the oven for 15 minutes or until the muffin is cooked thoroughly.

Chocolate-Dipped "Marshmallow"

CALORIES: 153
4:1 RATIO: 0.8 g CARBS

Makes 2 marshmallows

Marshmallow texture is closely replicated by using dried, powdered egg whites that have been pasteurized making them safe to consume without cooking. The "marshmallow" is not exactly the same texture as a traditional version, but may prove to be a suitable replacement for kids on the keto diet.

_____ 15.9 g coconut oil, melted
_____ 1.3 g hershey's unsweetened cocoa powder
_____ 2 g calorie-free sweetener, Truvia™
_____ 2 g dried egg whites, Deb El, Just Whites
_____ 1 tablespoon cold water
_____ 1.4 g gelatin, Knox unflavored
_____ 1 teaspoon hot tap water

Optional: 5 Total drops of vanilla and chocolate flavors, Bickford™

Measure all ingredients on a gram scale. Dissolve the gelatin in the hot tap water in a small bowl. Set aside to allow time for the gelatin to soften. Mix the cocoa powder with the coconut oil, 1 g of the Truvia™, and optional chocolate flavoring and pour into two silicone cupcake liners or similar size candy mold. Make sure that all of the chocolate mixture has been scraped out of the mixing bowl. With an electric hand mixer, mix the egg white powder with the 1 tablespoon cold water until a light and fluffy texture is achieved. Blend the remaining 1 g of Truvia™, softened gelatin, and optional vanilla and marshmallow flavorings into the egg whites. Scoop the egg white mixture on top of the chocolate and gently pat it down. Make sure that all of the egg white mixture is scraped out of the mixing bowl. Place into the refrigerator to allow the gelatin to "set" the marshmallow. Gently remove the marshmallow by sliding a silicone scraper along the sides and then by pressing on the bottom to release the chocolate. Place the marshmallow sides together to make a sandwich-style cookie or serve as is. Store in a plastic baggie in the refrigerator until ready to serve.

Homemade Dairy-Free Yogurt

CALORIES: 153
4:1 RATIO: 2.7 g CARBS

Each batch makes seven, 5-oz servings.

This recipe requires special equipment, a yogurt maker, and a food thermometer. They are not expensive and well worth the money and time if you would like to enjoy a full 5-oz serving of dairy-free yogurt! The benefit of this process is that the yogurt is actually cultured with the beneficial bacteria found in yogurt.

_____ 570 g coconut milk, Thai Kitchen, unsweetened, full fat
_____ 274 g almond milk, Blue Diamond Almond Breeze, unsweetened
_____ 3 g agar agar flakes, Eden Foods, crushed into powder
_____ 26 g coconut milk-based yogurt, so delicious, vanilla flavor
_____ 10–15 drops of vanilla flavor, Bickford™

Measure all ingredients on a gram scale. Pour the coconut milk, almond milk, and agar agar flakes into a saucepan. Heat on medium heat, stirring very well until the mixture reaches 160°F and the agar agar has dissolved. Turn off the heat, cover the milk mixture and let it cool until it reaches 95–110°F. Whisk in the coconut milk yogurt and vanilla extract. Make sure that the yogurt is fully incorporated into the milk mixture. Pour the mixture into the yogurt jars and culture in the yogurt maker according to the specific yogurt maker directions. This recipe has been tested with a 10-hour culturing time. When the yogurt has finished culturing, seal the containers and place the yogurt in the refrigerator.

Notes: Sterilize all the jars and utensils prior to using to kill any bacteria. The agar agar is not necessary in this recipe; if you omit it, it will result in a yogurt "drink."

Although there is a lot of inactive waiting time for this recipe, the actual prep time is very limited. This recipe can easily be incorporated

Homemade Dairy-Free Yogurt (*Continued*)

into a busy day. When cooking dinner, approximately 6 p.m., heat the milk mixture to 160°F. Allow it to cool while you are eating, cleaning up, and putting the kids to bed. Test the temperature several times, but it should cool down to 100°F within 2–3 hours. Mix in the starter culture and pour into the yogurt maker, set the timer for 10 hours, let it culture overnight. When you wake up in the morning, the yogurt will be ready to go in the refrigerator.

Do not be tempted to move the yogurt around once it is in the yogurt maker. This will affect the consistency of the finished yogurt.

Dietitian's Corner: Yogurt contains healthy bacteria, such as *lactobacillus*, which have been known to help promote a healthy digestive tract. Our bodies require a certain amount of healthy probiotic bacteria to help fight off harmful bacteria. *Lactobacillus* also helps the body to digest lactose, so it is beneficial for people with lactose intolerance.

Index